PEARL S. BUCK
Good Earth Mother

Pearl S. Buck

PEARL S. BUCK
Good Earth Mother

by

Dr. Warren Sherk

Foreword by
Julie Nixon Eisenhower

Drift Creek Press

1992

Printed in the United States of America
Designed by John Bennett
Frontispiece portrait by Hank Richter

Library of Congress Catalog Number 92-071740
ISBN 0-9626441-3-7

Dedicated to
the memory of my friend

Pearl S. Buck employer, mentor, friend

and to the Amerasian children sponsored by the Pearl S. Buck Foundation

Contents

❧

Foreward   ix
Preface   xi
Acknowledgments   xv

Chapter 1. Growing Up In China   3
Chapter 2. Education   27
Chapter 3. First Marriage   39
Chapter 4. Mother's Death   45
Chapter 5. Life in China   59
Chapter 6. First Books, Father's Death   65
Chapter 7. Furlough to America   73
Chapter 8. Certain Turmoil   79
Chapter 9. Marriage to Richard Walsh   85
Chapter 10. *Asia* Magazine Book Shelf   91
Chapter 11. Nobel Prize   105
Chapter 12. Green Hills Farm   113
Chapter 13. East and West Association   127
Chapter 14. Welcome House   141
Chapter 15. Vermont   153
Chapter 16. Richard Walsh's Death   161
Chapter 17. Pearl S. Buck Foundation   169
Chapter 18. The Final Years   179
Epilogue   187

Appendix
   Welcome House and the Pearl S. Buck Foundation   195
Bibliography
   The Works of Pearl S. Buck   201
Index   217

ILLUSTRATIONS

Pearl S. Buck drawing frontispiece

Rev. and Mrs. Absalom Sydenstricker 13

Absalom Sydenstricker 14

Pearl Comfort Sydenstricker as infant 15

Pearl at age 8 and sister Grace 16

Pearl's Mother, Grace and Pearl 31

Richard Walsh 67

Mr. and Mrs. Walsh, Janice & four adopted children 101

Pearl Buck and the King of Sweden 109

Green Hills Farm 117

Pearl's office 117

Main library 118

Dining room 119

Living room 119

Barn 175

Pearl Buck at age 80 183

Final resting place 183

Pearl Buck chop 185

Dr. Warren Sherk and Pearl Buck stamp 191

Foreword

⚬

As the child of missionary parents, Pearl Buck, the only American woman to be awarded both the Nobel and Pulitzer Prizes in literature, knew the pain of feeling different. Her light blue eyes and blonde hair made her forever a foreigner: "…I grew up in China, in one world and not of it," she wrote, "and belonging to another world and yet not of it."

As Dr. Sherk points out so clearly, Pearl Buck's early years opened her eyes to human suffering and instilled an intense interest in and curiosity about other peoples.

She became a champion of the downtrodden, particularly the Amerasian children, half-Asian, half-American outcasts in their own countries. Pearl Buck recognized no color or cultural barriers. She founded Welcome House, the first adoption agency to focus on the needs of racially mixed children, and the Pearl S. Buck Foundation, the dream of her later years, which still assists the Amerasian children.

Pearl Buck was a humanitarian, a prolific writer of over eighty books, mother to nine adopted children, an accomplished pianist and sculptor. Her life was so full that she once admitted to her friend Ernest Hocking that her existence had "been like trying to drive to capacity, and yet in an orderly fashion, a team of too many horses." Pearl Buck succeeded at whatever she put her hand to, and the author of this biography has brought into sharp focus the immense richness of her life.

JULIE NIXON EISENHOWER

Preface

ﾠﾠﾠﾠﾠﾠﾠﾠﾠﾠﾠﾠﾠﾠﾠﾠﾠﾠﾠﾠﾠﾠﾠﾠﾠﾠﾠﾠﾠﾠﾠﾠﾠﾠﾠﾠﾠﾠﾠ۰

Ifirst met Pearl S. Buck in the early 1940's when I became involved in the India League of America. Pearl Buck and her husband Richard Walsh were the honorary presidents of the League. I had just returned from a year's studies in Burma and India and was well aware of India's social and political problems. I attended every important lecture and meeting pertaining to Asia and spoke on every possible occasion about these countries, trying to interest Americans in their problems. Since I was already a confirmed Asiaphile, when Pearl and Richard founded the East and West Association on broader interests than India alone, I did all I could to foster its beginnings, finding places for its speakers to make addresses and stages for its performers. Thus our common interests caused our paths to cross more than once. I would see her, for instance, at the New York Town Hall Forum, which presented Krishnal Shridharani, Anup Singh, General Carlos Romulo and many others of the Asian leaders of that day.

Pearl Buck spoke out when American citizens of Japanese descent were interned in Japanese relocation camps during World

War II. I, too, was horrified and managed to be the first to obtain the release of one of the detainees. With the help of the young people in a western New York church, I got him a college scholarship. This same young man repaid our country more than in full by acting as translator in the war trials. He later invented the ceramic material that is used in the nose cones on American space vehicles to withstand the terrific reentry heat.

All of these Asiatic interests intersected with those of Pearl Buck, and I began to receive Christmas cards and an occasional note of greeting from her. In the post-War years I took a teaching post at Iliff School of Theology in Denver and couldn't attend the functions in New York City as I had before. Even then, each time Pearl Buck was in the area, she would contact me via a short phone call and we began a regular correspondence.

When she invited me to New York City in 1948 to discuss an "idea" she had, I was nearly penniless for I did not make much as an educator and spent every cent I had in trying to foster the ideals in which I believed. The only way I could possibly come, I explained, would be if she could wire me the money first, which she promptly did. Her "idea" turned out to be a position as Field Secretary for the East and West Association. My job would be to sign up artists and speakers from China, Korea, the Philippines, India, Burma and Indonesia for tours in the United States. (This was the worthy forerunner of President Eisenhower's "People-to-People" program.)

The day I was scheduled for my appointment, Pearl's outer waiting room contained the Ambassador to China from the United States, the Honorable Charles Leighton Stuart; the Vice President of China, the Honorable Mr. Li; James Yen, founder of the Chinese Mass Education Movement; and a wealthy Maharani from India. Irrespective of the waiting dignitaries, Pearl directed her secretary to escort each one to the libraries or other rooms, where refreshments were served. She then gave me her full attention and an unhurried interview.

Her plain, business-like dress belied the plans, programs, ideas and projects which she discussed animatedly with me. She indicated that we would have to operate on a shoestring budget. I was able to oblige by taking advantage of the offers of friends and, although quartering on the East Coast, I could spend part of the year on the West Coast following through on my many contacts there.

Her graciousness and altruism won me completely. In order to keep their *Asia* magazine and their own personal writing as objective as possible and free from undue influence, Richard and Pearl never accepted the paid trips and benefits they might have enjoyed from heads of state. They personally underwrote *Asia* for as much as $100,000 a year rather than accept any financial backing that might have jeopardized their freedom to tell it the way it was. This very freedom was soon threatened by Senator Joseph McCarthy's ill-advised attempt to label anyone as Communist who had an interest in the affairs of other countries. They were eventually forced to give up the East and West Association, and I was obliged to find other employment. Nevertheless, we continued to correspond, and I treasure the letters she wrote to me over the remaining years of her life.

This is a story of an age long gone, of ideals crushed by political ambitions. All of Pearl Buck's energies were channeled into finding relief for the children who were the unfortunate consequences of liasons between native women and soldiers stationed in foreign countries. As I served on the board for the Foundation she established before her death, I began to realize that those who knew her personally were getting fewer and fewer. I determined to write this book before all who had known this great woman in the prime of her life had passed away.

Thus I began a fifteen-year quest for the personal touch for this story. My search for friends of Pearl Buck led me to many wonderful people, and I found myself working on the manuscript as I travelled from border to border; in Arizona, at Lake Mohonk, New York, along the shore of Lake Erie and aboard the ship *SS Rotterdam,* where I nearly lost part of the manuscript overboard while on a lecture trip from New York City to South Africa.

At long last I met Craig J. Battrick of Drift Creek Press, whose faith in my story made it possible for me to share my knowledge of Pearl S. Buck with large numbers of readers, at a time when we desperately need to re-examine her attitudes and feelings about East-West relations. This book would never have been possible without his imaginative approach and gentle editing. Thank you, Craig!

Craig, in turn, introduced me to his book designer John Bennett, craftsman *extraordinaire,* who lent his artistic talents to the design of this book. Thank you, John!

While we were in the final stages my wife Jean spent many, many hours validating and adding to the known list of Pearl Buck's writings, a task that proved to be unending as even up to the deadline she kept finding references to short stories and articles not on any existing list. Thank you, Jean!

This is a selective and not a definitive biography as Miss Buck was so prolific that it will be a while until anything like a definitive biography can appear. Thank you, Pearl S. Buck!

Corvallis, Oregon   W.S.

Acknowledgments

↝

ARIZONA - Mary (Mrs. Jerry) Bartlett, Richard Bietz, D.D.S., Jim and Maxine Greenwood, Carolyn Kleck, Bob Petley, Hank Richter, Helen Root, Ph.D., Al Wilson and Al Yee.

CALIFORNIA - Dom and Carol Arthur DeLuise, Jim De Saegher and Malcolm Willits.

CONNECTICUT - Maureen Corr and Marge Linse.

FLORIDA - Martha Parker.

NEW JERSEY - Mary Roebling.

NEW YORK - The archivist staff of the Oriental Division of the New York Public Library: Mrs. Usha Bhasker, Dr. John Lindquist and Mrs. Samantha Murthy; the archivist staff at Franklin Delano Roosevelt Library, Hyde Park, and Rachel Smiley.

OREGON - Dona Beattie, Bob Burtner, Kathy Greey, Fred and Ruth Harrison, Lee Rudisill, Ruth Shirley, Diana and Ray Tufts, Laura Weaver, Deborah Wydronek. Many thanks to my publisher and editor, Craig J. Battrick.

PENNSYLVANIA - Marie Bauers, Lois (Mrs. David) Burpee, Jan Coughenour, Julie Nixon Eisenhower, William Fenn, Florence and George Galla, Sumi Mishima Gerhart, Julie Walsh Henning, Very Rev. George and Martha Kemp, George and Esther Loos, Betty

✒ ACKNOWLEDGMENTS

McConnell, Marie Miller, John Shade, Marion Sanborn, Helen (Mrs. Warren) Shaddinger, Charles Solomon, Grace Sum, Janice Walsh and the Welcome House staff.

TEXAS - George and Jan Lockhart and Eun Ha Ko.

VERMONT - Jackie Breen and Fred Carmichael.

WEST VIRGINIA - The staff of the Pearl Buck Birthplace Foundation, Hillsboro.

CANADA - Dan Bailey and Audrey and Ernie Maskell.

Special thanks to Janice Walsh for permission to quote from published works covered by the family trust.

I would like to thank my wife, Jean, for her total, indomitable, concentrated efforts to assist me all the way through this long effort.

PEARL S. BUCK
Good Earth Mother

Growing Up In China
⤙ CHAPTER 1

To two generations of readers the world over, Pearl S. Buck seemed to be the embodiment of China. If one were to weave together the tapestry of her China novels alone, he would have a picture of a time, a country and a people unique in the annals of literature.

Yet, of all her parents' children, Pearl was the only one not born in that fabled land of temples and pagodas.

Absalom and Carie (Caroline), were back in the United States on a year's furlough from his calling as a Southern Presbyterian missionary when the child arrived. It was their first trip home in ten years. So Pearl Comfort Sydenstricker first saw the light of day June 26, 1892, in her mother's family home, the Stulting Place, in Hillsboro, West Virginia.* Carie chose the middle name Comfort because she hoped that her first child born in America would compensate for the three babies she had buried in

* The house, begun by Carie's father, still stands today, high on a hill near the picturesque Allegheny Mountains.

the Foreigner's Cemetery at Shanghai. "He shall carry the lambs in his bosom," she had carved over their single grave.

After the birth, lying there in her own room with its peaceful view of the distant mountains, Carie could savor her pleasure to the full. Nothing in her bedroom had changed. Her clothing now hung in the same deep closets where as a young girl she had kept her hooped skirts. Her wide and comfortable bed was canopied with the same flowered muslin curtains. It was a beautiful room by any standard, but as she lay quietly with the new babe in her arms, she thought often of the three she had lost.

"You do not bear these little children," Carie once told her husband. "You do not understand what it is to give your life to the making of a child and then see it die. Don't you understand, it's myself dying."

Despite the hardships, Carie felt fulfilled. Young women of that era were raised on the stories of Ann Hasseltine Judson, who in 1812 became the first American woman to serve in Burma. For them, marriage to a missionary was the epitome of good fortune and sacrifice. Carie was no exception. In her youth she had never really come to grips with God, so when Absalom asked her to share his life in the service of others, she quite believed that God had called her at last.

Pearl's birth into a missionary's family meant that religion would play a crucial role in the development of her outlook on life, much as it had in the lives of her ancestors. The original Stultings had fled their native Holland to escape religious persecution, while Carie's mother had been a French-Huguenot. Likewise, the Sydenstricker ancestors had left their German homeland in search of religious freedom.

Absalom Sydenstricker grew up in a family of seven sons, six of whom became ministers. Pearl would one day write of her father's family: "Religion was their meat and their excitement, their mental food and their emotional pleasure. They quarreled over it as men quarrel over politics."

Their quarreling did not go unnoticed, for a local journalist labeled them "the preachingest family in Greenbrier County, with dissenting blood as strong as lye." Five of Absalom's brothers were loyal Southern Presbyterians. The exception was Christopher, who, "in the madness of his rebellious youth," joined the Methodist Church. The dissent didn't stop there, however. At age sixty, their mother Deborah joined Christopher and became a Methodist, to the great astonishment of their father.

Absalom's mother had made him promise that he would take a wife before embarking for China on his lifework and right from the beginning, Carie would come second to his work. When the young bridegroom made travel arrangements for China, she discovered that in his excitement he had purchased only one train ticket to the West Coast. As Pearl would one day recall, "He had a wife, but he never could quite remember it."

Carie soon found out that this man whom others called a saint could still be humanly sensuous. It seemed that every time he returned from his itinerant travels through the Chinese countryside, another baby was soon on the way. "My children have been my great romance," Carie often said. But Absalom, whose life was wrapped in a mystic union with God and the souls of men, never really learned how to share in the life of home or children.

They stayed four months in Carie's family home after Pearl was born. The blonde baby was welcomed by her mother's cousins who each day bathed and helped care for her. When she left with her older brother Edgar and their parents for China, the cousins cried that they were losing their treasure.

Once aboard the ship Carie was plagued by seasickness and nausea to the point that her milk soured and she was unable to feed the hungry infant. Absalom, who really did not care for children (his own or any other), tried to give Pearl a bottle, but she utterly refused it. In desperation, and with the help of a friendly stewardess, they took turns spoonfeeding the baby from a cup.

As they neared China, Carie remembered the first time she had glimpsed her adopted land. They had travelled from San Francisco to Japan on the rickety old ship *City of Tokio* then completed the journey on an old-fashioned sidewheeler. She expected the same picturesque, craggy shores that she had seen in Japan but instead was faced with the muddy yellow waters of the mighty Yangtse River as, unyielding, it flowed boldly into the clear blue sea.

This time, when they docked in Shanghai, Wang Amah, their Chinese nanny, was there to meet them. The Chinese woman first hugged Edgar to her breast, then took the new baby into her arms, laughing and crying at the sight of this child. Not yet six months old, Pearl had already travelled 10,000 miles.

The little family lingered long enough for Carie to visit the graves of her lost babies. There she planted a white rose cutting she had carried, wrapped in damp moss and earth, all the way from her old garden in America. The huge palm overhead would shelter it from the burning Chinese sun.

They travelled by steamer up the Yangtse, then by junk along
the Grand Canal until they reached their home in
Tsingkiangpu.* As the sick and the poor stood at the mission
gates to welcome them, Carie recalled that the first time she had
come to China, it had been for God's sake. But this time she had
come for them.

Carie differed from her Absalom. His very life was given
exclusively to the saving of souls ("the Work," he called it) while
hers was dedicated to caring for the sick, the young and the
dying. Always searching for that elusive Holy Grail, and blessed
(or cursed) with a saint for a husband, to please him—she often
prayed, "God, help me to remember that souls are more than
bodies." As she applied sulfur ointment to the running sores on
the bodies of the children in her classroom, it was difficult to
think only of their spirits.

Carie's ministrations to the poor soon caused her to become
known as "The American of Good Works." She was helped by
Wang Amah** whom she had rescued from a life of squalor
and despair. One day Carie had heard weeping as she passed
the hovel in which the woman lived. Wang Amah had given
birth to a daughter, but in those days Chinese men were
allowed to kill their newborn baby girls. As the child had suck-
led at its mother's breast, the Chinese woman's male companion had come in and crushed its skull. Carie took the woman
into the mission house and saw that her baby was properly

---

* Carie hated travelling by junk. She could not forget the time she had awakened below
deck to find a rat entangled in her hair.

** Amah means nanny.

8 buried. In return, Wang Amah rewarded her with years of love and devotion.

Only once was a quarrel heard between Carie and Wang Amah, the root of which could be found in the vast difference between the cultures of the United States and China. Carie ordered young Edgar to tidy his room every day and to carry in wood for the fire. To Wang Amah this was unthinkable. The elder son of the house was being forced to do the work of a servant! While the family ate, the Chinese woman quietly made Edgar's bed and tidied up for him. When Carie's eagle eyes later looked into the bedroom, there was nothing with which she could find fault. Edgar said nothing.

Then one day Carie discovered their secret. Lashing out in Chinese, for she now had a command of the language, Carie warned Wang Amah that she would brook no interference with her children. However, it was Wang Amah who had the last word. "It is a shameful thing in our eyes to make the eldest son work. For the girls, yes, it is well, but not for the sons." Although Carie was soon sorry for her outburst, her Chinese friend never could comprehend the strange customs of her beloved Carie.

At Wang Amah's funeral, Carie was the one who would speak her epitaph: "I believe Wang Amah was what people call 'not a good woman' and I am afraid she will never understand very much of the gospel. But I have never seen her be unkind to one of the children, nor have I ever heard her speak an evil word, and if there is no place in heaven for her, she shall have half of mine—if I have one."

Little Pearl grew sturdy and strong on alien soil. Her first memory was of toddling down the garden path, holding tightly to Edgar's hand, toward the gate that opened onto a busy street. It was always locked. This gate was hung six inches above the ground, so that the inquisitive two-year-old needed only to fall on her chubby knees to peep out. She was rewarded with a glimpse of long robes and muscled legs. Then, turning around, she saw her mother in a long white dress and an old straw hat with a gay red ribbon holding it in place. Carie was carrying a pair of shears, for she was a great gardener. She soon cut a large bouquet of the white roses that clung to the gray mission house, then allowed both children to smell their fragrance and feel the cool drops of dew that covered their petals.

Pearl could also remember the anxious time later when her mother lay white and listless for three long months from a severe attack of dysentery. It was Wang Amah who cared for the children, religiously combing Pearl's blonde hair, all the time teaching the child Chinese nursery rhymes and singing her native melodies. When Pearl was ready, Wang Amah marched her in for her sick mother's inspection. Wang Amah loved Pearl as her own, although at times the girl-child's independence and curiosity amazed her.* Sick or not, there would soon be another baby. Absalom was out on some lonely highway saving souls when their new son was born. He had blue eyes and black hair, an interesting combination, Carie thought. She named him Clyde.

Absalom liked to wear Chinese clothes, including a round black hat with a crimson button on top. His Chinese shoes had to be specially made to cover his enormous American feet, about

---

* The relationship between the two was so close that Pearl called Wang Amah "Foster Mother."

which the Chinese women loved to giggle over and make jokes. As his daughter would one day write: "He had had adventures enough to fill books and had been in danger of his life again and again." Absalom reminds one of Robert Morrison, the first American missionary to China in the 19th Century. When a sea captain asked Morrison, who was still a young man, whether he thought he could make any kind of impression on China, the missionary politely replied, "No sir, but I expect God will."

Being a missionary was no picnic, for as a Southern Presbyterian, Absalom had plenty of competition from the missionaries of other denominations. They often caused him more trouble than the people he had come to save. It was trying for him to have made a good Southern Presbyterian convert one year, only to return the next to find that the man had been immersed as an equally good Baptist!

China was ruled at that time by the Empress Dowager Tz'u Hsi of the crumbling Manchu Dynasty, a woman with a fascinating past. Known first as Yehonala, she was the imperial concubine of the Emperor Hsien Feng. When the Emperor died in 1861, their son became the new ruler. Yehonala and the Empress Consort Tz'u An became Empresses Dowager in an edict made in the name of the infant emperor. Aided by Prince Kung, Hsien Feng's brother, they overthrew the established regency.

Yehonala, now officially known as Empress Dowager Tz'u Hsi, schemed to control the throne. When the boy emperor, T'ung Chih, died in 1875 (officially of smallpox but more likely of the dissolute lifestyle in which Tz'u Hsi had seen fit to encourage him) his widow conveniently committed suicide.

Then, in 1881, the other empress, Tz'u An, died. It was rumored she had been poisoned.

Now only Prince Kung stood in Tz'u Hsi's way. Prince Kung conducted most of China's diplomacy with foreign countries (from 1860 to 1884) and although he was her best statesman, she hated him for taking part in the execution of her favorite eunuch. She stripped him of his posts and thus gained full control of the Manchu throne. The Empress Dowager replaced Prince Kung with her new favorite eunuch, Li Lien-ying, whose nature was as corrupt as her own.

The next emperor, Kuang Hsu, came of age in 1889. The Dowager Empress relinquished her regency after first marrying him off to her own niece, whom she clearly expected to carry out her government policies. When Kuang Hsu implemented his own plans for radical reform, the Dowager Empress first arranged to have him murdered. When the plot was foiled, she had him imprisoned. Again she took the helm of state, sailing blindly into catastrophe. She hated all foreigners, missionaries especially, and labeled them troublemakers. Into this atmosphere of potential violence Absalom had thrust his family.

Absalom considered Chinese magistrates and fellow missionaries his enemies. He was frustrated with the former, who impeded his work, and unpopular with the latter, who thought him too educated. When Absalom let it be known that he was translating the New Testament into Chinese, some of his competitors were green with envy.

It was the unwritten law between the other missionaries to stand together when it came to those they dubbed "the natives."

12 If a missionary quarreled with a convert or Chinese Christian preacher, the white man was always in the right. Otherwise, in their misguided opinion, "to allow the natives to undermine the authority of the missionary, what then would happen to the authority of His church?"

The missionaries were jealous of Absalom's indefatigable energy for God's work, but most of all, as his daughter said, "they wanted to be rid of his sympathy for those whom he had come to save." Absalom loved the Chinese, confessing, "I've learned bitterly that I can trust them more." Believing a Chinese before one of his own kind became the principal complaint made by other missionaries against him. They even wrote to the Southern Presbyterian Board of Foreign Missions to complain about him. Fortunately, that august body knew Absalom's real worth, so he continued to go his own way.

The Chinese had a long history of distrusting foreigners, not just those from a far country, but even from another province. Such interlopers were often buried alive. But Absalom was the most obstinate of men. When a magistrate refused him permission to preach in a particular town, Absalom reminded him of foreign treaties negotiated after the Opium Wars that allowed the missionaries to preach and the Chinese to listen.

To aid his travels, Absalom designed a wonderful wagon and built it with the aid of a Chinese carpenter and a blacksmith. An enormous crowd gathered to watch the latter beat out the springs on his anvil. Absalom bought a mule, hitched it to his new contraption and was ready to go. It certainly was an improvement over his own legs or the little donkey he often rode. Unfortunately, the wagon's fame went before it, and like the

Rare photo of Pearl Buck's parents, Rev. and Mrs. Absalom Sydenstricker.

"The Fighting Angel"—Pearl Buck's Father, Absalom Sydenstricker.

Pearl Comfort Sydenstricker as an infant.

Pearl at age 8 holding her baby sister Grace.

Prodigal Son in a far country, Absalom was set upon by a band of robbers. They threw all of his tracts and Bibles into a ditch before making off with his clothes, mule and cart. He walked the thirty miles back to Carie in his underwear. At the mission house, she dressed the cuts on his head, for Absalom had put up quite a fight.

Later Absalom appeared before the local magistrate, a friendly old scholar who sat placidly smoking his opium pipe, and demanded the return of the mule and wagon. After Absalom made his usual threats of international sanctions against those who mistreated missionaries, the magistrate, who knew his persistence, managed to have the cart returned. It was quite ruined Absalom never did get his mule back, for, as the old magistrate apologized, the robbers had eaten it.

Absalom decided that his wagon had been sheer earthly vanity, so he returned to riding the lowly donkey, emulating his Lord. He travelled the highways and byways, perfectly happy with no companion but God. He carried a large stick to ward off the packs of half-wild dogs that he encountered until, in time, even they grew used to him and ceased to attack.

Of her father Pearl would write: "I may as well confess, I was afraid of Absalom," but added, "I know that Absalom never meant to frighten a little child or dreamed that he did."

The fear of her father was not entirely of his making. Carie had been brought up with the maxim "Spare the rod and spoil the child" but she could never quite bring herself to carry out the punishment. It was always left for Absalom to perform such unpleasant tasks on his rare visits home. Once when Clyde was little more than a toddler his father smacked him for some minor infringement, but the little chap, still weeping, managed to sing the first verse of "Onward Christian Soldiers." All her life, Pearl could not sing the familiar hymn without recalling that incident.

Ironically, red letter days for the family occurred in the spring when Absalom, like a latter-day St. Paul, started off on his journeys. His bedding roll was prepared complete with mattress, homespun blanket and pillow, for there were always lice in the beds at the inns. The roll was thrown across the donkey, then Absalom, armed with sun hat and dog stick, straddled the sturdy little animal, his long legs only two inches from the ground. Everyone shouted, "God speed," and he was gone.

At once a sense of calm descended on the bustling mission house. Carie sat at the precious organ her brother Cornelius had sent all the way from West Virginia, playing her favorite hymns and singing. As twilight fell, she told the happy children, "We'll skip prayers tonight and take a walk instead—just for once God won't mind."

Pearl fell asleep before she had said her own prayers that night. Awakening the next morning, she realized she was perfectly safe. God had not punished her for being remiss, as her earthly father had said He would. Later, she said, "I never feared Absalom quite so much again."

One winter Carie nearly lost Clyde with pneumonia, for the earthen house with its thatched roof proved extremely damp. There was no doctor for hundreds of miles. With Wang Amah's help she made a blanket tent around his bed where cold drafts could not penetrate. For ten days they nursed him until he was out of danger.

When Absalom came home, Carie and Wang Amah had everything packed and were ready to leave the house. Before he could even open his mouth, she announced, "You can preach from Peking to Canton, you can go from the North Pole to the South, but I and these little children will never go with you again. I shall take them to Chinkiang to that bungalow on the hill, and if it is empty, we will stay there where there is peace and where there are hills and fresh air. Otherwise I go back to our own country. I have offered up three children. I have no more children to give away to God now."

And go she did. Absalom, for once, followed meekly behind. But he never really forgave her.

Pearl learned to speak Chinese before she knew English. Having already mastered Chinese when it came time to read and write, she studied English rather than the difficult Chinese characters. She maintained throughout her life that her first writings were thought out in Chinese, then translated into English.

Very early she discovered the world of books. She read anything and everything she could find because reading brought to her new people, new places. Pearl remained a voracious reader throughout her life. She also absorbed lessons from the teeming multitudes around her, watching people gardening, sowing, setting, weeding and harvesting. She loved the flow of life. At about the age of six, she informed one of the families at their summer cottage in Kuling that when she grew up, she was going to have an enormous house and fill it with thousands of babies.

As Pearl grew older, she became acutely aware of the "Saints and the Sinners" as her father called them. She did not always understand the significance of the stories about them until she was older. Her mother tried to protect her from the more common life about them, but she couldn't protect her from hearing the screams of the Chinese girls and women far into the night whenever the sailors came ashore on leave. She also was aware of the mixed breed of children around her, who were called British-Asian, Franco-Asian or Russo-Asian.

Sinning was not restricted to the sailors. Even those Chinese who practiced polygamy were sometimes shocked when a bereaved missionary took another wife almost immediately. One story concerned the infidelity of an old man who didn't wait for his spouse to die. This sweet old white-bearded fellow and his wife were retired from the mission field. It seemed he had taken a young Chinese woman as his concubine. He even prayed with his long suffering wife over the sad situation. But she, good woman that she was, decided in her heart that her wandering spouse was like Abraham and she the aging Sarah who urged him to take the younger Hagar for his own.

Whenever Pearl travelled on the river with her parents and Edgar, they saved money for the printing of Absalom's precious Chinese New Testament by putting on Chinese clothes and travelling below deck with the Chinese. The sweet, sickly smell from the pipes of opium users filled the darkened salon while the clatter of bamboo dominoes continued day and night. The family ate bowls of rice and cabbage ladled out of wooden buckets plunked down on the floor. Dessert was rice pudding with prunes. Carie washed the children liberally with a carbolic lotion in an effort to ward off bedbugs and lice.

The lusty Yangtse River captains were mainly English by birth. They indulged in profanity, good Scotch whiskey and missionary baiting. Absalom was always fair game for the captain, whose favorite theme was obscenity in the Bible. "It's got more dirty stories in it than you can find in any other book. Corruptin' the heathen, that's what it is."

Once, their father turned red, then snapped at the captain, "He who reads aright, reads to the salvation of his soul, but there are those who read to their own damnation." While this exchange had been going on, Pearl and Edgar were so intent on watching the captain that even their sharp little eyes failed to notice a pickpocket steal their father's watch and precious fountain pen!

At five, little Clyde came down with diphtheria. Carie sought the help of two doctors, a kindly Anglo-Indian whose medical skills were minimal and the British customs doctor who was always so drunk that nobody ever knew if he was really competent or not. Carie sent a Chinese runner to fetch Absalom from the field, but he arrived home to find his grief-stricken wife mourning the death of her youngest child. It was so wet the day of the funeral that Carie, ailing herself, was unable to go. The scene of her mother weeping by the window as the small coffin passed on its way to the Foreigner's Cemetery was engraved forever on Pearl's small heart.

But there were happy times too. As Christmas approached, Pearl and Edgar would work for weeks to make something "pretty" for their mother, who all her life craved beauty. (They would wince on Christmas morning when their father gave her some trivial gift wrapped in nondescript brown paper, because as Pearl was to write: "He did not know what she liked or what she wore or what she needed!" He always managed to spoil everything, saying nobody knew exactly when Christ was born, which prompted Carie to exclaim, "Fiddlesticks, Absalom. The point of it is to give the children a good time.")

Ordering from the Sears Roebuck catalog was the most exciting of all their childish pleasures. Each child could choose something costing a dollar, the dollar going much further in those days. Then the great day came at last when the coolies brought the wooden boxes of goodies swinging from ropes attached to their carrying poles. There was everything inside, from tins of coffee to a round keg of molasses for the tasty gingerbread that Carie made. There were even the inevitable suits of long underwear with which to combat the long Chinese winters.

When the order arrived, they could have a little party for the children who came to the mission, especially the little half-white, half-Chinese that nobody except Carie wanted. That was how Pearl first came to know these little ones. When she grew up, she did not forget.

At fifteen, Edgar was sent home to America to finish his education. All that he knew he had been taught by his mother who, sad as she was at seeing him go, believed it was time he learned how to live among his own people. So she commended him to the care of her brother Cornelius. Pearl was the only child in the house for a time. Then another little daughter, Grace, was born. Again, the mother nearly died, for the white doctor's remedies did not seem to help her. It was Wang Amah's fish broth, long used by the Chinese to combat puerperal fever, that finally saved her.

Pearl was lonely with Edgar gone and no children her own age with which to play. But fate was kind. A young woman whom Carie had befriended died, leaving a ten-year-old child named Precious Cloud. On her deathbed the woman begged Carie to raise the child as her own, which she did. She called Precious Cloud "my Chinese daughter," while Pearl called her "my sister." In spite of the Chinese custom of binding the feet of little girls, Carie adamantly refused to do so. Instead she had pretty embroidered slippers made for the child. Carie was happy with her little girls.

In 1900 came the Boxer Rebellion. Pearl was then eight years old. The wily old Dowager Empress, fearing that the Japanese and various European powers were trying to obtain additional concessions and privileges in China, ordered that all foreigners be killed. The missionaries were the first to suffer. A number were murdered and their churches burned.

On January 18, the Americans, British, French and Germans sent notes to the Dowager Empress and her government, decrying the violence and murders of their missionaries. This only angered the Empress more. As a result, she called upon the members of a society known as the Righteous Uniting Band to join her imperial armies and get rid of the hated foreigners.* The German minister, Baron von Kettler, was murdered, as was a secretary at the Japanese Legation.

At the mission house Carie was ready for any emergency. Food for baby Grace, extra shoes and a change of underwear for every-

* This society, whose name was mistranslated as "Righteous Uniting Fists," became known in western papers as the Boxers. Thus, the conflict was called the Boxer Rebellion.

body were rolled into a bundle to carry with them should they have to flee. The American Consul, who lived in what was known as the Bund, had warned them that should danger be imminent, he would fire a cannon and dip the Stars and Stripes three times. When the ominous signal finally came, the little family, along with Wang Amah, made their way through the bamboos to a steamer waiting by the river. At the last minute Absalom refused to go, saying that his first duty was to the Chinese Christians. As the steamer set out for Shanghai, he could be seen dressed in white and wearing a pith helmet, standing with his converts on the wharf.

For the next ten months, Carie, Wang Amah and the children lived in a Shanghai boarding house. Pearl and Precious Cloud were kept busy with their lessons. Pearl, like her parents, loved to read, and she knew many Bible stories by heart.

At last the eight foreign powers organized an international force, destroyed Chinese forts and occupied Tientsin. The legations were relieved just in time to avoid the massacre ordered by the Dowager Empress, who in shame and disgust disguised herself and fled to Sian, the ancient capital in China's Northwest. She took with her the captive Emperor, and when his favorite consort, the Pearl Concubine, meekly suggested that he should have been left behind to negotiate peace with the foreigners, the Dowager Empress had her flung down a well for being impertinent.

When the rebellion ended, the Dowager Empress returned to apologize to the hated foreigners and grant fresh concessions. No longer would Pearl and Grace be required to pray, "God, please keep our father from the Boxers."

Suddenly, Absalom appeared in Shanghai to announce that they were all going to America for a year's furlough. Now Pearl would actually see the big white house in which she had been born. She would meet her Grandfather Hermanus, the silver-haired patriarch of the family, and her Uncle Cornelius. Best of all she would have cousins to play with.

Once in America, Pearl felt "glorious and free." She became used to a house with no walls to enclose its garden. Later she wrote: "I became convinced bandits would not attack us or come in and steal our things."

It was also a time of awakening. For the first time she realized what a good sermon her father could preach, for he was much in demand in the local churches. When her grandfather was shocked that Absalom had walked fifteen miles over Droop Mountain carrying a suitcase after his horse had gone lame, Pearl was filled with admiration for her father that she had never known before. "There're always books in his suitcase, too," she told everybody.

In 1905, when Pearl was thirteen, the crops failed in China; famine fell over the land. Starving country folk poured into the cities, looking for food that was not forthcoming.

Absalom went to the North where the famine was most severe to see that money sent from the faithful in America really was spent in providing food. Carie did her part at the mission home. With the little money that Absalom managed to send her, she bought food to distribute to people starving in the streets. She forbade desserts in her own home. Instead of celebrating Christmas, their happiest time, she invited her children to help cook great vats of rice to feed the hungry. She would no longer shield her daughters from the real world beyond the mission walls. The wailing voices of the sick and dying could not be stilled.

With joy Carie received a shipment of food from America, only to find that it was comprised of cheeses, something the Chinese found sickeningly nauseous. Then she had an idea. With the help of Pearl and Wang Amah she peddled the cheese to foreigners and bought needed rice with the proceeds.

Thus, Pearl's education continued, not alone in books, but also in the practical realities of life in China. As she grew in physical stature, her understanding and love grew through her service to the Chinese people around her.

Education

Pearl's education at her mother's hand continued in spite of revolution and famine. Carie made her elder daughter write a composition each week and study music and painting. Pearl was happily surprised when her first writing was published in the Shanghai newspaper's children's page when she was ten years old. As she grew, her little pieces were published frequently and she sometimes even won prize money for them.

The precious organ that Cornelius had sent his sister several years before was used for other things besides hymns. Pearl was required to learn to play it as part of her home curriculum.

Along with these studies, Carie imbued in her daughter her own love of beauty and order, traits that had been prominent in Carie's father. Thus, beauty and order were inextricably molded into Pearl's writing and lifestyle. But along with the studies exacted of her, she was allowed to follow where her own curiosities led her. She later remarked that she had the "chance to know the delight of long days, empty except for what one puts into them, where there is nothing to do except what one wants to do. No wonder I was a happy child. I was never overcrowded and rushed with unnecessary things."

Carie's view of Pearl was different. She thought her daughter's nature was much like her own, compassionate and lonely. The memory of people dying in the street for lack of food seemed to make Pearl nervous and distraught. Carie decided to send her to a boarding school for girls run by two New England spinsters in Shanghai. Both her parents spoke highly of Martha and Eugenia Jewell, who had founded their school for missionary daughters. After two years, Pearl would be ready for college in America.

The young girl arrived at the Shanghai school in a dress that an accommodating Chinese tailor had copied from an American magazine. Unfortunately that same tailor hadn't the slightest idea as to how to make a young lady's hat. Never mind, Carie had a box full of old hats and even ball gowns and corsets sent by well-meaning, pious Americans to help clothe victims of the famine. Of course they had been useless, yet the ever resourceful Carie could not bear to throw anything away.

"Try to pretend we went to Paris and bought you a chapeau," she told Pearl, who was not at all sure she wanted a famine hat. However, after she watched her mother steam and press the offending dark green creation, good manners prevailed. She accepted it graciously.

Pearl found the school downright gloomy with its barred, prison-like windows. The Misses Jewell seldom smiled; they were both firm disciplinarians.

Outspoken, Pearl upset her roommates by announcing there

really wasn't much difference between Buddhism and Christianity. Did they think perhaps that the Lord Jesus had borrowed His golden rule from Confucius?

They didn't! In shock, the other missionary daughters reported Pearl to the Misses Jewell, who decided that before she further contaminated her roommates with heretical reasoning, Pearl would be reassigned to a room of her own. There, she was in her element. When everyone else was officially sleeping, she could read in bed.

Like her father, Pearl excelled in literature, English and philosophy. The Friday Literary Club thought her different but interesting. She was even, so she said, writing a novel. They could not understand why, by her own confession, she read Lewis Carroll's *Alice in Wonderland* for what she described as its "deeper insights."

The Misses Jewell insisted their students help at a rescue home known as the Door of Hope, catering to former slaves and prostitutes. Pearl would never forget the cruel and hair-raising stories that these unfortunates told her. She soon became aware of the many Chinese of mixed blood living in Shanghai, unwanted and unloved. Their blue eyes haunted her, and at night she dreamed of them.

Pearl would have liked to have chosen Wellesley for college, but her mother would have none of it. "Why, that's a northern college," Carie protested. Finally they agreed upon Randolph-Macon Woman's College in Lynchburg, Virginia, a college that had Methodist-Episcopal affiliations instead of their own Southern Presbyterian. There were several factors in its favor. It was inexpensive and featured as full a curriculum as a male college. In addition, her brother Edgar, now married and father of a little daughter, worked for a Lynchburg newspaper.

It was time for Absalom and Carie to take another furlough. They went home so that Pearl, now seventeen, might be settled at her new college. First, however, there was to be what she called "the great battle of Father's New Testament." It was also the only time that Carie, with great determination and show of temper, forced him to postpone his long-planned next edition. Pearl heard her parents arguing behind their closed bedroom door. Then her mother appeared with face flushed to triumphantly announce, "I am going to get you that other dress after all, child, and we are going home by Europe."

The Sydenstricker family took a steamer up the Yangtse River, then by rail from Hankow to the north. It took ten days to cross Russia; they all shared the same sleeping quarters with Pearl and Grace sleeping in the upper bunks. The facilities were primitive. Carie produced a basin for them to wash in while the toilet was simply a hole in the floor at the end of the passage. An ever resourceful provider, Carie had also brought along canned milk, home-made jam, coffee and other niceties. Hard-boiled eggs, cheese and black bread could be bought every time the train stopped.

Russia displeased both Pearl and her mother, for the wealth of the ruling class contrasted the sheer poverty of the peasants. Carie prophesied, "These people are going to make a revolution one day that will shake the world." Pearl wrote, "I felt a fearful premonition of a world to come; the innocent would suffer because of the anger of an outraged people."

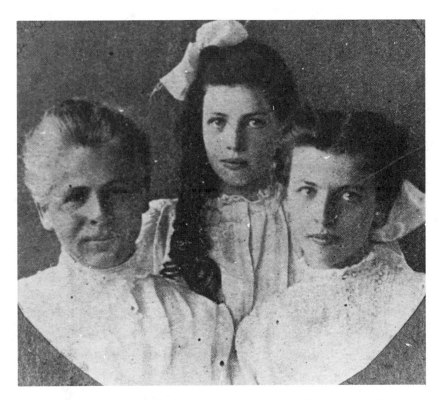

"The Exile"—Pearl's Mother, with Daughters Grace and Pearl.

Somehow Carie had scrimped enough for them to spend two wonderful months in Switzerland. Ever eager to make the best use of her time, Pearl studied French and German from private tutors, eventually using these two languages in her research in medicine and science.

When they visited France, Absalom enjoyed touring the cathedrals and castles, but the Paris museums were another story. The nude statues offended his modesty.

The Sydenstrickers enjoyed England where mother and daughters decided the people were so in love with their Royal Family that there would never be an uprising to change anything, as they feared in both Russia and China. Taught by her mother to love her native America, Pearl discussed with Absalom the good that Americans had accomplished in China, building schools and hospitals. Absalom was not so sure, telling her: "We missionaries went to China without invitation and solely from our own sense of duty. The Chinese therefore owe us nothing. We have done the best we could, but that was our duty and so they still owe us nothing. And if the United States had taken no concessions, we have kept silence when others did, and we too have profited from the unequal treaties. I don't think we shall escape when the day of reckoning comes."

These were words that Pearl never forgot.

Once in America, the family first visited relatives in the big white house where Pearl had been born, but her parents were no longer comfortable there. Carie missed her small, arrogant, white-haired father. Since his death her brother Cornelius and his wife had become master and mistress of the family home. Down in the village, Absalom's brother had also died; a strange minister filled his pulpit. Finding such changes, Absalom and Carie were glad to move on to Lynchburg and their son Edgar's home. Unfortunately they did not care for his wife, Alice, who was not intellectual, but Carie did enjoy the company of her grandchild. "The baby," Pearl said, "was a delight to her."

With both parents in attendance, Pearl arrived at Randolph-Macon Woman's College, travelling by interurban streetcar. After registration, they kissed their daughter goodbye and then left her wearing her dress of Chinese grass linen, unlike anything worn by the other students. While many girls had small, artificial curls in their hair, Pearl's was worn in a braid swept severely up at the back. She described herself as "slender...an eager, shy, childish creature, full of contradictions and in many ways strangely mature." In most ways, she did not fit in.

The first night at supper she saw more American girls at one time and in one place than she had ever seen in her life. Only one other new girl bothered to speak to her, and that was Emma Edmunds, who, raised in a small village, was feeling pretty lonely herself.

Fortunately, as long as her parents remained in America, Pearl was allowed to spend her weekends with them. Her mother was not well, so she dreaded their return to China. In church, during the hymn "America the Beautiful," she saw that her mother was weeping. "Oh, America, America," Carie kept repeating. It was as if she knew she would never see it again.

One church service Pearl would never forget for her father had been asked to preach in the college chapel. When he marched in behind the president wearing his old-fashioned gray suit, giving at the seams and of an obsolete cut, she wanted to crawl under the pew.

Pearl's feelings were not helped by the southern drawl of a fellow student, "He looks as though he'd be right long-winded."

Blood being what it is, thicker than water, Pearl snapped in a hurt voice, "He's my father."

"Oh, I am sorry," said the southern girl with obvious embarrassment.

"It doesn't matter," Pearl conceded. "He is long-winded."

Pearl had tried so hard to understand Absalom, but she finally reached a reluctant conclusion. "Great missionary he was, intrepid soul, but there was no fatherhood in him.... His children were merely accidents which had befallen him."

Autumn passed and Christmas finally arrived. This would be the last holiday she would spend with her parents for four years. But unlike previous Christmases, this one was a disaster. Absalom remained distant and insensitive. Edgar and his wife squabbled all the time. Pearl was actually glad to get back to campus.

Pearl shared her room at college with one other girl. It was peaceful, if spartan, and contained two single iron beds, one gas burner, one bureau, and two hard chairs. Each bathroom had three bathtubs, which had to be shared by twenty girls obliged to make advance reservations.

Attendance at chapel was compulsory, as was gym, where the girls wore black serge bloomers, black stockings, white blouses and black ties.

From her first lonely college day, Pearl realized two things. She was not like the other American girls. She would have to make herself become like them. And she had to dress as they did if she were to be less obvious.

Pearl earned money by coaching backward students. Then she went to "the best shop in town" to buy the new clothes she needed. By the end of her first year, she proudly wrote, "I was indistinguishable from any other girl of my age and class."

Her academic courses did not phase her. She would always do well with them. Her professor of freshman English could hardly believe how well-prepared she was. A college myth perpetuated for years that Pearl had failed her freshman English course is simply not true.

The college library was her true home as, a generation before, it had been her father's. Her happiest hours were spent tracking down subject after subject. In fact, for one whole year her private reading at the library was her chief pursuit.

She longed for the innate beauty of natural settings, and early on discovered the nearby James River, often visiting it with other students. She took nature walks to maintain a healthy mind in a healthy body and to nourish her love of beauty and order. To satisfy her ever-present curiosity, she asked questions, questions, questions, not about the unusual, but about the daily routines of life which others found boring. The answers to these questions were to fill volumes that would later delight her faithful readers. One of her professors wrote, "It was as if the soul behind the eyes was looking and recording impressions as they came into being."

On weekends she still visited Edgar and Alice, a duty that she hated for their marriage was fast disintegrating. During her second year she joined the college literary societies; she was made a member of the Student Committee, became class treasurer, and then, in what she always called her "greatest triumph," was chosen by a senior to be "attending squire" at the graduation. When

36   the Kappa Delta sorority pledged her (and they were on record as not being too fond of intellectuals), Pearl Comfort Sydenstricker knew that she had finally been accepted as their peer. No longer would they snicker about "that awful girl from China."

One spring a letter came from home—for China was her home—with the terrible news that her beloved Wang Amah had died. Pearl said of this Chinese woman, who was in effect her second mother, "She left her share in us, her white children. Part of her went into us, as mothers are part of their children, so that now and forever her country is like our own." Pearl wept as she remembered Wang Amah's "faithful brown face, wrinkled and toothless under her scanty white hair."

There was more family sadness to come, for Edgar confided to his sister that he was contemplating a divorce from Alice. Would she please tell their parents? In an era when divorce was considered a cardinal sin, this was no easy request. After receiving the startling news, Carie sent back a tear stained letter. She wished, she said, that she had never allowed Edgar to leave home so young. Sensitive to his mother's suffering, Edgar actually did not divorce his wife until after the deaths of both his parents.

Pearl was to represent the college at the YWCA conference at Bryn Mawr. She assumed the presidency of the Franklin Library Society, the Senior Club and the Modern Literary Club. She was also a delegate to the Student Volunteer Movement's quadrennial meeting at Richmond, Virginia in 1912.

She was loathe not to accept one honor that she badly wanted, editorship of *The Tattler,* for Edgar had begged her to stay with

Alice while he took a post in Washington. Only boarders could be editor of *The Tattler,* but as she had always loved her brother Edgar, she went to stay with his unfortunate wife. However, several of her stories and verses had been well received in the college magazine's pages. Her fictional short story, "The Hour of Worship," told the story of a woman missionary whose faith had been lost. It was reminiscent of Carie's unresolved dilemma.

At year's end Pearl won the two most cherished prizes for best story and poem. She was quite hurt at the jealousy shown by some of her fellow seniors, who felt that she should not have been awarded both prizes.

Only her brother and one cousin were present at her commencement exercises. The traditional phrase following her listing in the college yearbook, *The Helianthus,* consisted of the words "SKY PILOT." Underneath was the symbol of a candle between two crosses. This symbol was prophetic of what she would do throughout her life through her innumerable books and by the quiet example of letting her light shine in a steady glow of humanitarian acts.

Pearl was undecided about returning to China after she finished her schooling. She never hesitated to speak her opinion that "China will never be won to Christianity except through those who know and love her." Following graduation Pearl was offered an assistant's teaching post by her psychology professor, which she was thrilled to accept, only to get the dread news that her mother was desperately ill with sprue, which affects the red corpuscles in the blood. Immediately she decided to go home and asked the Southern Presbyterian Board of Missions to find her a teaching post in Chinkiang, which they were only too pleased to do. She left for home in November of 1914, the year that World War I began. It was not the best of times to be travelling, but she reached China within a month.

The voyage home was made all the pleasanter because of a brief shipboard romance with a young man from the Standard Oil Company who was ten years her senior. She admitted this to be "the first time I ever kissed a man with all my heart." Pearl bragged of how he "nearly proposed," asking her to go with him to Manila. She declined, and they went their separate ways.

She was met in Shanghai by her father and Grace, who had grown into a pretty young woman. They travelled by train to Chinkiang, where her sick mother was eagerly waiting. It was a happy reunion, for the soft boiled eggs, liver, fresh fruit and gruel which the doctor had recommended for Carie seemed to be helping.

And for the first time in her life, Pearl's thoughts turned to the serious possibilities of romance.

First Marriage

China had gone through drastic changes since the old Dowager Empress's passing in 1908. It now had a great new leader, Sun Yat-sen, a Christian doctor turned revolutionary. In 1912 he became Father of the Republic of China. Pearl, now teaching in the mission school, was both "stirred and stimulated."

One thing was missing, however, and she was worried, for unlike the Chinese, Carie and Absalom had given little thought to their eldest daughter's marriage. Absalom thought she should seek a Chinese husband, but Carie did not.

Pearl, who had enjoyed four stimulating years in her native land, was determined to find a suitable American. In time she did.

His name was John Lossing Buck. He had been born in 1890 on a farm near Poughkeepsie, New York, of Dutch, British and French ancestors. His parents were simple, industrious people who had brought up their four sons, of whom John Lossing was the eldest, to follow the same mores.

40   Lossing, as he was known in the family, had worked his way through Cornell Agriculture College. He became interested in foreign missions through a group that met on Sundays at the college religious center. There he began a friendship with Hu Shih, a fellow agriculture student who would one day be honored by his government with the Ambassadorship to the United States. Hu Shih stimulated Lossing's interest in China.

After graduating in 1914, Lossing spent a year showing young reformatory inmates improved farming methods, after which he decided to serve as an agricultural missionary in China. Dr. Henry Sloan Coffin, pastor of the Madison Avenue Presbyterian Church in New York City, interviewed Lossing and liked what he found. His church's China project included a mission post at Nanhsuchou, where most of China's wheat was grown.

Lossing arrived in Shanghai in June of 1916. He immediately enrolled in the University of Nanking's School of Languages in order to learn Chinese. He lost no time in seeking suitable female companionship, for on July 26 he wrote his mother that he had just met "a nice missionary's daughter."

Her name was Pearl Comfort Sydenstricker.

Pearl was naturally attracted to Lossing. He was good-looking, auburn-haired and tall, and he commanded a salary of fifty dollars a month as well. He courted her with long walks, teas and chaperoned picnics. In turn, she took him to meet Carie and Absalom at their summer home in Kuling. The meeting was far from successful. Afterward Pearl admitted that her parents were "vigorous" in their joint disapproval of Lossing Buck.

Carie and Absalom were intellectual snobs when it came to education, so Lossing's agricultural degree did not impress them.

Pearl was not to be swayed by their feelings, for she saw in Lossing a certain honesty and kindliness. Besides, she was twenty-four, which to the Chinese side of her upbringing was terribly old for a woman to be husbandless.

Unfortunately, she failed to realize that her father and Lossing were much alike. The former was only interested in being a missionary, while agriculture, according to a close associate, was Lossing's "whole life."

In due time Lossing proposed and Pearl accepted. When her parents protested, she informed them bluntly, "You are behaving like Chinese parents. You think whomever I marry has to suit the family first."

Carie had the last word which, in the years to come, her daughter would have good reason to remember. "This is a mistake," her ailing mother said. "You will be sorry. We know you better than you imagine. How can you be happy unless you have someone who understands what you are talking about? He never reads and you are never without a book."

Love, as usual, was blind, so on May 30, 1917, Pearl married John Lossing Buck in the rose arbor of her parents' home. The ceremony was Presbyterian with sister Grace serving as the bridesmaid. Pearl wore the customary white bridal gown with veil and held a bouquet of Carie's roses. Her younger sister, raised to be a frugal missionary's daughter, was somewhat shocked by all the expensive Shanghai lace with which Pearl had trimmed her trousseau.

The Bucks started their married life in what Pearl described as "a lovely little Chinese house" in Nanhsuchou, nestled in the shelter of the city walls. "There were four rooms," she says, "but what pleasure to arrange the furniture, hang the curtains, paint a few pictures for the wall, hang the Chinese scrolls! I was happy and busy."

Emulating Carie as a good correspondent, she dutifully wrote Lossing's mother every week with details of their daily doings. Typing these letters made her more proficient at helping her new husband with his growing business correspondence.

"Mother," she wrote, "Lossing has a great future before him here. I try to help him all I can…. We are happier all the time." She begged her mother-in-law to send the recipe for Lossing's favorite whole wheat bread.

Pearl's quest for knowledge of the people they served was insatiable; there were plenty of adventures to write home about. Once she went with Lossing to inspect a mission station some sixty miles away—he on his bicycle, she carried by four coolies in what she calls "a very uncomfortable chair." Sometimes Lossing got far ahead of Pearl and her entourage. When she did not appear, he backtracked only to find her sedan chair surrounded by an enormous crowd of people who had never seen a white woman before. They touched and laughed at what to them was a long nose and big feet. At an inn, where they were given the stable for sleeping quarters, they found the smell of manure to be far from pleasing. Out of friendly curiosity, the crowd nearly pushed in the door, so Lossing pinned sheets over the windows to ensure their privacy.

Sun Yat-sen's new Chinese government was far from stable, and this provided additional excitement. Once, during a skirmish by local warlords outside their home, Lossing was almost hit by a stray bullet.

After three years in Nanhsuchou, Lossing was abruptly told by his Presbyterian employers in New York that his agricultural project was cancelled. Fortunately, Dean John Reisner of Nanking University, who was developing a new Agricultural Economics course, invited Lossing to come and help him. It was at this time that Pearl found herself pregnant. When unforeseen complications arose, her doctor sent her to Nanking, where she lived with Dean Reisner and his wife Bertha, who was also pregnant.

Pearl's baby was expected in the latter part of December or early January. She had joked that it would surely be born on Christmas Day, but Christmas passed and New Year's Day, too, without the longed for child's appearance. Finally, on March 20, 1921, a daughter, Caroline Grace, to be known as Carol, was born. She weighed seven pounds and eight ounces.

Coming out of the ether, Pearl saw first a pot of budding plum blossoms and then her baby wrapped in a pretty pink blanket. "There is a special purpose for this child," the nurse insisted, and in the years ahead, Pearl would often recall her words.

Mother's Death
⤙ CHAPTER 4

P earl did not recuperate as quickly as expected following the birth of her baby. Her physician, Dr. Horton Daniels, diagnosed a tumor in her uterus. Drastic treatment in America was necessary, so with Lossing and baby Carol she left for his family home near Poughkeepsie. Grace had been attending a Tennessee college, but periodically came to look after her baby niece when Lossing's mother was unable to do so.

Surgery was performed on July 10 in New York City's Presbyterian Hospital. Although the tumor was benign, the doctors decided during the surgery to perform a hysterectomy. Pearl was told afterward that she could never have another child. She was twenty-nine years old.

Pearl returned to Nanking with Lossing and Carol the following November. There she enjoyed a much larger house and garden. It was fortunate that Lossing earned a good salary. College students visited frequently and the Lossing Bucks were able to employ a male cook, an amah for the baby and a gardener who also ran messages.

The extra help gave Pearl much needed time to care for her family. Baby Carol suffered from a recurring and unsightly form of eczema. In addition, Pearl felt doubly responsible for the care of their ailing mother, now suffering from pernicious anemia.

Pearl once arrived at Carie's to find her mother in her best lavender dress, chewing a wad of gum. "Well, here you see your old mother, chewing gum," she quipped. "I hear it's the latest thing in America."

Carie and Absalom's home was two hundred miles away, and the need to provide constant treatment for Carol's eczema as well as care for her mother finally proved to be too difficult to handle alone. Pearl was obliged to call Grace home from college to help.

Upon Grace's arrival they determined that Carie needed professional care, so they sent to Shanghai for a nurse. The respondent was an English woman of uncertain age whose ravaged face was covered with makeup, and whose hair was colored blonde with peroxide. Normally such a visage would have been anathema to Carie, but her bright eyes were dimmed with disease and now she saw only beauty.

"Why is that pillow case on your head?" she demanded.

"I will take it off if you like," answered the startled nurse, removing her cap.

"Why, what pretty hair you have, my dear, hid away like that," Carie exclaimed, "and so lovely with your fair skin."

The English woman was quite taken back; it had been years since she had known such genuine compliments. Carie won her instant devotion. To Pearl and Grace, in those last sad days, the nurse became a godsend. No patient knew better care. In turn, Carie was good for the nurse, listening to her life story with gentle sympathy, even when at times it was quite sordid. "I know how hard it is to be good, especially when no answer comes," Carie told her.

With Carie in the nurse's care, Pearl returned home. But it was only for a short time. When it was obvious that their mother was failing fast, Grace sent for her again. Pearl arrived to find Grace and the English nurse trying to fox trot to a jazz tune played on their old Victrola. Carie had begged to see how it was done.

"Well, that's a pretty thing, so graceful and light," she managed to say. "I should not be surprised if Absalom is all wrong about God. I believe one ought to choose the happy, bright things of life, like dancing and laughter and beauty. I think if I had it to do over again, I would choose those instead of thinking them sinful. Who knows? God might like them." Having made her point, Carie fell into a light sleep.

She did not forget Absalom in her last days, for she knew him too well. She warned her daughters, "Look out for spring. About the first of April he gets hard to manage. It won't matter if he's eighty, he'll get away over the country and behind the hills preaching."

Carie died in her sleep on an October afternoon. Her daughters dressed their mother in her best lavender silk gown, then placed golden chrysanthemums around her. Pearl could not cry; she touched her mother's hand and said, "It is like marble."

48   Carie was buried beside her little son Clyde in Chinkiang's Foreigner's Cemetery on a pouring wet day. Later Pearl wrote in an epitaph for her mother, "To the thousands of Chinese whom she touched in every sort of way she *was* America." But on her mother's funeral day, she could only think of the old Chinese proverb, "When the tree falls, the shade is gone."

Absalom's was a strange grief; unless asked a direct question concerning Carie, he never spoke her name again. After the funeral he locked himself in his room, where Pearl, peeping through the window to make sure he was all right, saw him hard at work on his New Testament, carefully painting the Chinese characters one under the other. Nevertheless, in his heart he must have missed Carie, for as Pearl noted, "There was now no one at home to contradict him, blame and scold him into energy."

As we have already seen, Absalom had upset some of the younger missionaries—the "righteous young men," as Pearl so aptly called them—by siding with the Chinese in disputes. The missionaries in turn had written long reports full of complaints concerning him to the missionary board in America. Back came a new ruling: missionaries must retire at age seventy. When they brought Absalom his resignation, he signed it without a word.

Spring came, and just as Carie had prophesied, Absalom became restless. Soon he was off on his old white horse again, ministry or no ministry. Along the road he saw a bamboo grove, and there, like his Lord before him, he went in to pray, begging to be forgiven for his "sin of despair." He found his churches closed and shuttered, the Chinese preachers he had trained with such care had been dismissed and scattered to the winds by those same "righteous young men."

When Absalom confronted them, they said he was dividing the church, and as for his founding an independent church, it was sheer folly if not heresy. Finally they threatened to send him back to America. Pearl realized that she must act quickly before her father's heart and pride were broken. She appeared in person before the mission board without his knowledge, suggesting he might operate a correspondence school for them in Nanking. Some board members were difficult, but in the end Pearl triumphed, and they invited her father to form the correspondence school just as she had suggested. She then moved him and Grace from Chinkiang to her own home in Nanking.

Punctually every day Absalom went to his office. Evenings he ate supper with his despised son-in-law, to whom he never spoke. Lossing suffered in understanding silence.

When he first came to live with them, Pearl gave Absalom the largest and best room in her home. Facing both the mountains and an old pagoda, each morning it was filled with sunlight. She furnished it with the pretty rug from Carie's sitting room, simple white curtains, Absalom's favorite chair with a cushion, his books and the clock he had wound for forty years. On the single iron bed he had bought for himself, she placed an extra mattress.

But the next morning she was dismayed to find that he had stripped the room bare as a hermit's cell. The rug was rolled up and pushed under the bed. Even Carie's picture had been taken down and hidden. Absalom, Pearl conceded, "had his own monastic way to the end."

In a scene reminiscent of her mother's life, Pearl was one day confronted by a pregnant Chinese woman of unkempt appearance who asked, "Do you remember me?"

Apparently the woman had been the wife of the Buck's gardener in Nanhsuchou, Mr. Lu. In a time of famine, her husband had deserted her, then their five children had died in the uprising called the "Ten Day Madness."

Mrs. Lu begged that she might live in Pearl's chicken house until her baby was born. By this time, she declared, she knew all there was to know about having babies. When her time came, she would need no help.

Pearl found the woman a hut, small but bigger than the chicken house, had it properly cleaned, then furnished it simply. She left iodine, bandages and a pair of scissors for the birthing.

In due time a baby boy was born. Because of his chubby cheeks, his mother named him the Chinese equivalent of "Little Meatball." When Mrs. Lu poured the entire bottle of iodine on to his small belly, she burned him quite badly. Little Meatball was rushed to "Wise Mother," as Mrs. Lu fondly called Pearl, who in time managed to heal him.

The healing process had to be repeated later when Mrs. Lu decided she was tired of using the diaper cloths that Pearl had given her. The old Chinese way of laying a baby on the sand certainly seemed much easier, but as she had no sand, so Mrs. Lu used cool ashes instead. Unfortunately, when the urine mixed with the ash it turned into a powerful lye, badly burning Little

Meatball's bottom. This time it took a good two weeks for Pearl
to heal the unfortunate child. Grateful Mrs. Lu, as future events
were to prove, never forgot Pearl's patience and kindness.

In the midst of such domestic activities Pearl S.
Buck, then thirty years old, decided she was ready to fulfill a
repeated threat: she would become a writer. On an August
afternoon, dressed in her best blue silk, Pearl wrote an essay
entitled "In China Too" which she mailed to the *Atlantic
Monthly*. Seen through the eyes of a Chinese matron, it compared her daily life with American women about whom she
had only read. The story was accepted and printed in the
January 1923 issue.

Gradually Pearl slipped into a regular writing schedule. The
activity seemed to fill a growing void in her life. Over time, the
love she had once felt for Lossing had diminished. They had little
in common and were gradually drifting apart.

Pearl was also increasingly worried about Carol, whose growth
and progress was not as it should be. She noted that Carol burst
into tears at the least provocation, while Pearl's friends commented on a strange look they seemed to see in the child's eyes.

One person who could get Carol to smile was Jesse Yaukey, a
young missionary who boarded with the Bucks while he attended
the Language School. Pearl was grateful to the patient man from
Pennsylvania who could bring out the best in her child. When
Jesse fell in love with Grace, Pearl gave the wedding in her living
room among tall pots of bamboo. After the wedding was over
and Grace had gone with her new husband to his mission station,
Pearl thought, Carie "would have been proud."

Carol's condition continued to worsen until even Pearl finally admitted that all was not well. "I think I was the last to perceive that something was wrong," she wrote of the sad situation. "I did not think of such a possibility."*

In 1924, Lossing took a year's sabbatical, and the break seemed heaven-sent to Pearl. She had just been advised by a visiting American pediatrician to take Carol to America for further diagnosis. Pearl sadly called it "that long journey which parents of such children know so well." She hired Mrs. Celia Steward, a Methodist missionary, as a housekeeper for her father, then sailed for America with Lossing and their unfortunate child.

While Pearl searched for the answers to Carol's medical problems, both she and Lossing worked on their Masters' degrees at Cornell University in Ithaca, New York. Lossing's study was of course in agriculture, Pearl's was naturally in English.

They were given a parsonage in which to live, where Pearl did the housework. Money was tight and since she needed a winter coat, Pearl set out to earn one. The result was her first acceptance from *Asia* magazine for the story "The Chinese Woman Speaks." It was about a young Chinese who returned to his ancestral home with an American wife. Pearl was paid a hundred dollars for her effort.

Later, even though the subject for her M.A. thesis was English essayists, Pearl also won Cornell's Laura L. Messinger Memorial Prize for a long article called "China and the West." Never had this

* One of the interviewees for this book told the author many years later she often saw Pearl patiently awaiting her turn for medical care for Carol at the Nanking clinic. She particularily remembered the tender and loving manner in which Pearl chatted to the child and kept her amused.

prize been won by someone other than a graduate student in the history department. Even her own English professor had advised her not to try for it. The more-than-welcome prize was two hundred and fifty dollars, which she knew would be helpful in paying for Carol's medical consultations. The article was so thorough that years later she used it as the basis for a speech to the American Academy of Political and Social Sciences in Philadelphia.

At the Buck's home near the university campus Pearl came into contact with a large number of foreign students who, to her chagrin, were rarely if ever invited into American homes! It had become an obsession among foreign missionaries to send the most promising students to America for further study. However, these students often found it a very unchristian country when it came to hospitality.* Incidents like this were filed away in Pearl's mind, and perhaps had much to do with her later efforts to raise Americans' interest in those from other cultures.

That year in Ithaca was momentous for another reason. Eleanor Roosevelt, destined to become one of America's most popular First Ladies, had been invited to Cornell to speak. She arrived by train in Ithaca at seven in the morning wearing a purple evening gown, for, as she told Pearl, who was a member of the reception committee, she would have no time during the day ahead to change.

In her long satin gown, sensible oxford shoes and a hat that Pearl described as "nondescript," Mrs. Roosevelt was unique. She gave her speech to the Home Economics Department, then delighted her hosts by eating her seven-cent luncheon "with gusto." It consisted mainly of raw cabbage.

* This would change somewhat after the Second World War.

Like Pearl, Mrs. Roosevelt was uncommonly original in her approach to life. The two were destined to become lifelong friends.

Campus activities did not for one moment detract Pearl from her "long journey" to find help for Carol. Finally, one foreign-born doctor at the Mayo Clinic, more truthful than the others, told her the blunt truth: Carol would never be normal. She would retain a four-year-old mind all her life, and she would never walk properly. Carol was destined to live out her life in her own little world, far from reality. As Pearl left the clinic she felt as though she were "bleeding inwardly and desperately."

A previous doctor had suggested that a baby brother or sister would possibly help Carol; perhaps she was alone too much. The minister at Lossing's sponsor church, First Presbyterian in Troy, New York, heard of their search for a baby and took Pearl to visit a nearby orphanage. Adoption seems to have been easier in those days, for she was told immediately to select a child.

"I went from crib to crib," she explained. "At last I came to one where a very small, very pale little girl lay, her eyes closed. She seemed scarcely to breathe. 'How old is she?' I asked. 'Three months,' the director said, 'and she has never gained since birth. She weighs only five pounds. She will not eat.' 'I want her,' I said. He argued against it immediately. Why should I take a child doomed to death? But I insisted. I felt a strong instant love for the exquisite dying child. I took her in my arms and carried her away. The very next day she began to eat. In a fortnight she was so different, one would not have known her. She was actually plump."

What Pearl did not write was that the child was bald and her little face temporarily disfigured through having lain so long on one side. One ear had even grown in the wrong direction!

Pearl named the baby Janice and like Carol, she presented a great challenge; this time Pearl would win. Everybody at her in-laws' farm, including her visiting brother Edgar, admired her new daughter with the big brown eyes. Soon there would be a mass of golden curls to go with them.

Their year in America expired and the Bucks returned to China with their two toddlers. Brother Edgar, who felt in need of a change of scenery, accompanied them. Pearl lost no time reorganizing her home. Mrs. Lu had seemingly disappeared and new servants were soon found. Each had to be trained in his or her new duties and Pearl took great care to insure that these did not overlap.

Then one day Mrs. Lu reappeared with the sad news that Little Meatball had died the previous winter. The sympathetic Pearl hadn't the heart to ask her for details.

Mrs. Lu immediately asserted her place as part of the house-hold and asked for the job usually known as "table boy." She performed her duties with great pride until Pearl noticed with some concern that Mrs. Lu was rapidly gaining weight. Upon questioning, Mrs. Lu related how she had been seduced by a soldier while working in a field. Pearl couldn't quite imagine how such a strong personality could be "seduced" by anybody.

Again the long-suffering Pearl offered a little hut to Mrs. Lu, with whatever was necessary when her time came. It never did, for the woman suddenly decided that she did not wish to become a mother again. She performed a self-abortion for which she nearly paid with her life. Pearl had Mrs. Lu rushed to the hospital, where her life was saved. Again Mrs. Lu poured out her thanks to her "Wise Mother."

In the meantime, Absalom also became sick, so much so that he had to forego his correspondence school. At his elder daughter's suggestion, he set to work updating a book of Chinese dialects he had written.

Outside the Buck home, China was undergoing another period of upheaval. Sun Yat-sen, whom Pearl had admired since her childhood days, died in 1925. Carie had always believed in him, saying that "something good will come from Sun Yat-sen."

Sun's dream of a unified China was passed to Chiang Kai-shek, who became the new leader of the Kuomintang (Nationalist) party. Chiang inherited a daunting task. Not only was the Kuomintang split by internal rivalry, but Russian-backed Communists and "traditional" Chinese warlords in the North were also making bids for control of the country.

The land was also heavily infested with garden-variety bandits who took advantage of the confusion to pillage indiscriminately. The Yaukeys were victims of such banditry, and fled to Nanking to find safety with Pearl. At the time, Grace was pregnant with her second child.

The Nanking missionaries and other whites supported the Nationalists, believing them to be their friends. They had even cabled the State Department in Washington that they were in favor of "the Nationalists' principle of 'China for the Chinese.'"

Lossing apprised his missionary board in America of the latest developments in the struggle as viewed from Nanking. With con-

cern he noted that soldiers loyal to the northern warlords were
filling the city to confront Chiang's Kuomintang Army, which
was moving up on the city from the South. He assured those on
the board that looting was to be expected but that hopefully the
favored Nationalists could keep order.

Lossing, together with the other foreigners, was in for a rude
shock when the "Nanking Incident" occurred on March 24,
1927. It is now believed that Communist agents, dressed as
Nationalists, shot and killed Jack Williams, vice-president of the
university, then incited regular Nationalist soldiers to turn upon
all the other "foreign devils." The whites, of course, had no way
of knowing that the soldiers rampaging through the foreign sec-
tions of Nanking were being controlled by outside agents. They
felt betrayed by the Kuomintang whom they had supported. This
added to the horror of the conflict.

Mrs. Lu hid Pearl's extended family in her hut for thirteen of the most terrifying hours her "Wise Mother" would ever
remember. "I'm convinced that had it not been for that day, I
would never have left China, because my whole life was there.
On that day my cord to China was broken," Pearl later wrote. "If
I lived, it would have to be in the entire world."

She made the drastic decision that if the soldiers did find
them, she would not leave her two little girls to their mercy.
Before she died herself, she must first see them dead, adding
grimly, "even if I did it myself."

The children, small as they were, remained quiet throughout
the family's ordeal, as if in answer to their mother's prayers. The
faithful Mrs. Lu risked her life to bring bottles of boiled water,

loaves of bread and even a tin of milk for the little ones. Mrs. Lu also wrapped Pearl's aluminum saucepans in a quilt and brought them to safety.

Suddenly the flimsy walls of the hut shook with the thunder of cannon fire as American, English and Japanese gunboats swarmed into the river. The ordeal for Pearl's family ended when the foreigners were gathered together and escorted by the Chinese Red Cross to an American warship. Some of the Chinese openly apologized for the soldiers' actions, while others remained bitterly hostile to the whites.

The refugees were taken to Shanghai. There, Pearl's family separated. The Yaukeys left for Kobe to await Grace's confinement and Absalom departed to visit missionary fields in Korea. Pearl and Lossing went with their two small girls to the hot springs resort of Unzen, near Nagasaki, Japan.

Two months after arriving in Japan, who should appear at their door but the irrepressible Mrs. Lu, with all her worldly possessions secured in a kerchief. She had made her way to Shanghai and upon hearing that her beloved "Wise Mother" had left for Japan, she bought a boat ticket and set out after them. She did not know one word of Japanese, yet in the end she found Pearl Buck because, she explained, "I was sure you needed me."

Life in China

Pearl often wondered how her father was faring in Korea, but her worries were needless. As ever, Absalom was busy doing what he liked best—preaching. He had found groups of Chinese in Korea who had been neglected by missionaries that spoke only Korean. He was soon conducting services in the homes of the Chinese converts. In one letter he remarked, "It's extraordinary how the work lies waiting to be done."

Absalom was most critical of the Koreans. He did not like the way they dressed in their "silly clothes," the men in white linen shirts with tall black hats tied under their chins. He made the surprising comment, "Their souls seem scarcely worth saving." It was apparently twenty times easier to save a Korean than a Chinese, and the work had simply lost its challenge for him. As a result, Absalom was feeling homesick. In spite of the revolution, he longed to return to Nanking.

Word of events in China gradually reached Lossing and Pearl at their sanctuary in Unzen. Chiang Kai-shek, it seemed, had held talks with Western and Chinese bankers in Shanghai. He had turned against his Russian advisers and had sent their consul home. He was determined to crush the growing Communist party and anybody who supported it. Chiang Kai-shek even put a price on the heads of the Nationalist soldiers who had wreaked such havoc on the missionaries and other foreigners living in Nanking.

Since Mrs. Lu had unexpectedly arrived, Pearl was freed of many domestic duties and had time to turn her thoughts into notes for future writings. She turned even the horror of the Nanking Incident into a story called "The Revolutionist."

Lossing was writing, too. He had been conducting an extensive land use survey and his precious manuscript had survived the upheaval.* The writing, the interchange of ideas, the chance to "talk shop" brought Pearl and Lossing closer together. They were more compatible than they had been in years.

After some months in Japan, Pearl and Grace and their families safely returned to China. As Nanking was still overrun with soldiers, they chose to stay in Shanghai. In the French Concession of that cosmopolitan city they found a large, three-story house which they shared with a Chinese family. The Bucks lived on the top floor, the Yaukeys on the middle floor, and the Chinese family had the ground floor. The kitchen was shared by all.

---

* By summer's end of 1928, Lossing's survey was finished. It was published in 1938 under the title of "Land Utilization in China" by the University of Chicago. It made Lossing famous in the world of agriculture and to this day is highly regarded in The People's Republic of China.

One day, Pearl sent for Mrs. Lu to verify rumors of a domestic disturbance, something about Mrs. Lu keeping a young man prisoner in the house!

Incredibly, the rumors were true. It seemed that when the Buck family first left for Japan, Mrs. Lu had promptly fallen in love with this good-looking young man who was years her junior. Unfortunately, another woman also coveted him. The day before, Mrs. Lu had been buying vegetables in the open market when she saw the two together. Mrs. Lu was outraged! She virtually kidnapped the poor fellow, who wasn't very big, and despite his struggles, carried him home and locked him in the cellar.

In spite of Mrs. Lu's protestations, Pearl insisted upon hearing what the captive had to say. He bragged that both Mrs. Lu and the other woman wished to marry him. But, he concluded, since he could not afford to pay for the virgin bride, he would be glad to wed Mrs. Lu if she would only stop smacking him and treating him so badly.

Pearl had serious misgivings that a marriage based primarily on the wife's agreement to stop beating the husband would work out. But she finally gave the mismatched couple her blessing. Peace was again established in the kitchen.

But not for long, for the bridegroom turned up one day with the other woman, explaining that many Chinese men had two wives! This argument held no weight with Mrs. Lu, who was jealous because the other woman could bear him children while she, because of the self-administered abortion, could not. So she chased the other woman away and soon presented her new husband with the ugliest concubine she could find.

When, in time, the newcomer obligingly gave birth to a healthy baby boy, Mrs. Lu immediately confiscated him for her own. At last she had another Little Meatball.

On the top floor of the house in Shanghai, Pearl looked after Janice and Carol, aided by an amah. This took up most of her daytime. In the evenings she typed her stories and articles, determined more than ever to become a writer and earn the kind of money that would enable Carol to live at a special home in America. Since the Nanking Incident she worried about what would become of her retarded child, who would be left alone in China if anything should happen to Lossing and herself. There was still a degree of danger for whites living in China, and to make it worse, Lossing was making secret journeys to Nanking to continue work on his agricultural survey.

In 1928 Absalom returned from Korea, his tongue as caustic as ever. Fortunately for Pearl's writing, he preferred living with Grace on the middle floor.

It was about this time that Pearl wrote to two literary agents in New York City, seeking representation for her work. One replied by return mail that American readers were not interested in China. The other, David Lloyd, liked what she had enclosed, part of a short story called "The Chinese Woman Speaks." He decided that Pearl S. Buck could very well be an important literary discovery. She had explained to him in her letter that her manuscript could form the basis of a novel to be entitled "Winds of Heaven." Lloyd wrote back, suggesting that she finish her novel, which was all the encouragement she needed. It would be published in 1930 as *East Wind: West Wind.*

In time, the Bucks were able to return to Nanking and discovered that as the new capital, it now boasted all sorts of modern conveniences. It even had movie houses.

Their former home had been filled with soldiers who had stabled their horses in the rose garden that Pearl had planted with such love. Her typewriter had been stolen, but miraculously, there on a shelf was the manuscript she had written about Carie, her mother. Little did she think that in the years ahead it was destined to become one of her most popular books, *The Exile*.

The family soon planned another visit to America. This time Pearl was determined to find Carol a permanent home where she would be happy among other similarly afflicted children. She knew such a venture would cost money and she would have to earn it herself. Lossing was so frugal they didn't even have a joint banking account. He insisted that anything Pearl earned should be deposited in his account, much to the disgust of his colleagues' wives.

Pearl finally found a place known as the Training School in Vineland, New Jersey, whose genial director was Dr. Edward Johnstone.

"We have just one rule here," he told an anxious Pearl. "The children must feel happy and loved."

Unfortunately, the school cost a thousand dollars a year, but undaunted, she appeared before Lossing's Mission Board to seek assistance. One member of the Board was the wife of Dr. John F. Finley, Jr., the editor of the *New York Times*. Mrs. Finley was so impressed by Pearl's desparation that she convinced her husband to loan Pearl two thousand dollars, enough to allow Carol two years' stay at the School.

Before leaving China, Pearl had sent her literary agent, David Lloyd, the manuscript of the now completed "Winds of Heaven." But she hadn't told him of her new address in America. So he sent a cable to Nanking which finally reached her in Buffalo.

The message read:

> JOHN DAY OFFER WINDS OF HEAVEN SUBJECT CERTAIN CHANGES TEN PERCENT ROYALTY FIFTEEN AFTER FIVE THOUSAND ADVANCE PAYABLE ON PUBLICATION ADVISE.

Ecstatic, she went to New York to meet Lloyd, the man who would guide her frenetic literary career for the next twenty-five years. He, in turn, took her to the offices of her new publisher to meet its president, Richard Walsh.

This second meeting was significant beyond Pearl's wildest dreams. She had not only found a publisher, she had found her destiny.

First Books, Father's Death

From their very first meeting, Pearl S. Buck and Richard Walsh held a mutual respect for each other. He had an easy manner to which she reacted with candor. When she told him her age, he advised her not to reveal it, but she replied that it did not matter, for "in China every year is considered an additional honor." Accustomed to the Chinese philosophy that boys were more important, and usually better educated, than girls, she later said, "What was precious about Richard beyond jewels was the indisputable fact that he enjoyed my mind. We liked profound discussions on abstruse subjects. He enjoyed repartee. Most importantly, he accepted that I had to be alone when I was writing. He never asked what I was writing or even what the book was about. When it was finished, he would always say, 'This is a big day.'"

Richard Walsh's family had emigrated from Britain to Kansas where he attended public schools. He went on to Harvard

University, graduating magna cum laude in 1907. He had worked for the Boston Chamber of Commerce in public relations and as an editor for several publications including *Collier's* magazine. He was also the author of a commendable biography of the popular Indian fighter William "Buffalo Bill" Cody. When Pearl met him, he was married and had three children.

In 1927 Richard had raised the money to buy the John Day Publishing Company which, until that time, had produced mainly educational materials. He greatly expanded the publishing line and, unknown to Pearl, he was as delighted at finding so promising a talent as hers as she had been in his acceptance of her first novel. She was the woman he would mold into one of America's most popular women authors.

However, that was in the future. At present, Richard was forty-two years of age and had been forced to borrow his children's Liberty bonds to help with the worrisome financial state of his firm.

Ironically, he had been the twenty-ninth publisher to whom the agent had shown "Winds of Heaven." After seven weeks of deliberation, Richard sent his acceptance. He was to call it "the best decision I ever made in my life." Upon publication the book was retitled *East Wind: West Wind.*

Once back in China, Pearl lost no time and reactivated her attic writing room. There, before a window that faced the Purple Mountain, she began to work again. She had an obligation to write a juvenile book for the Mission Board that would pay off some five hundred dollars against the money she had borrowed for Carol's boarding fees. However, the book she had wanted to write for several years could be stifled no longer. She called it "Wang

Richard Walsh

Lung" after the peasant farmer who would serve as the hero. It took her three months to write, which included typing an extra copy of the manuscript. Without showing "Wang Lung" to anyone, she mailed it to David Lloyd, who received it in June, 1930.

Meanwhile, *East Wind: West Wind* had been published to generally good reviews. Encouraged, Pearl started a translation of the classic Chinese novel *Shui Hu Chuan* (All Men Are Brothers). Lloyd had sent her "Wang Lung" manuscript to Richard Walsh, who was ecstatic over its possibilities and he accepted it on the same terms as before. He then wrote Pearl to know if he might change the title, afraid that American readers might pronounce it "one lung." As an alternative, he suggested "The Good Earth." His author agreed. When she wrote that she had several other book ideas in mind, Richard Walsh was delighted.

He soon cabled to tell her that the Book-of-the-Month Club had made *The Good Earth* their March selection. Modestly, Pearl replied that although she was not a member of the club, she had noticed in the *Atlantic Monthly* its "very imposing list of well-known authors."

Then, complying with his request for a picture, Pearl found a Chinese photographer who took two pictures, one with Janice and another by herself. She received four thousand dollars, less her agent's ten percent commission, from the book club. She could now plan for the life annuity she wanted for Carol's security.

The Good Earth reached the bookstores on March 2, 1931, selling for $2.50 a copy. Some of her closest friends, including Emma Edmunds of her college days and now herself a missionary's wife, found it rather "coarse." Chinese intellectuals called it demeaning. But today, over fifty years later, *The Good Earth* is prescribed reading in many American high schools and has been for three generations.

At her home in Nanking, the author read the *New York Herald*   **69**
Tribune review declaring that she was "entitled to be counted a
first-rate novelist....This is China as it has never before been por-
trayed in fiction. *The Good Earth,* however, is much more than
China. This is the eternal struggle of men with the soil anywhere,
a struggle more stark and heavier with drama in China only
because there men fight with the will alone, unaided by mechani-
cal devices."

The Good Earth tells the poignant story of the peasant farmer
Wang Lung from the time he takes as his wife a slave girl from
the house of the Squire Hwang. They till the soil and beget their
children, eking out a meager existence until drought forces them
to flee southward, where Wang Lung keeps his family together
by working as a ricksha puller. Then, in the company of other
desperate people, they rob a rich family and with the loot are
able to finance the return home to the land they love. This time
the good earth prospers. The peasant farmer's sons are sent to
school, and as a mark of his new wealth and esteem in the neigh-
borhood, Wang Lung takes unto himself a concubine. He buys
the home of the Squire Hwang but finds little peace, for the very
sons he has educated turn away from the good earth that has
succored them. When he dies, they cannot wait to sell it to
become men of leisure.

When a bound copy of *The Good Earth* finally reached
her, Pearl particularly liked the blue cloth. Inside she could find
only one mistake: "fleas" had become "flees!" Suddenly she felt
very lonely, longing to share her achievement with somebody in
her own family. Lossing was out of the question, for he only had

time for his own agricultural writings. Then she thought of her father; surely, for once, he would praise her.

Absalom, who also liked the color of the cover, demanded to know how she had found the spare time to write it. He did glance at some of the pages but never read it properly.

Thank God for Richard Walsh; he always found time to write and report how her brainchild was doing. He also asked her to sign a contract that the John Day Company should publish her next three books. This she did gladly.

Back in New York, the Foreign Board of Missions soundly condemned *The Good Earth,* one member proclaiming that as a missionary's daughter and wife, Pearl was guilty of "unmentionable depravity." *The Good Earth* author held her ground, however, knowing that what she had written about the Chinese peasantry was the truth.

Richard's praise more than made up for the mission board's criticism. He wrote: "I cannot close without saying that my whole experience with you and your book has been just about the happiest and most wholly satisfactory I have ever had, not merely because it has proved financially successful but because I have been handling things of beauty and dealing with an author who is always considerate and understanding."

She in turn sent Lloyd the manuscript of her next novel, which she called "Sons." By this time both her agent and publisher realized that in more ways than one they had found in Pearl S. Buck a treasure.

Meanwhile the John Day Company submitted *The Good Earth* for the Pulitzer Prize, granted yearly for the best novel published by an American author.

In 1931, the mighty Yangtse overflowed her banks, flooding some fourteen and a half million acres. Millions perished in the Great Flood, their bodies floating aimlessly in the polluted waters, while others were left to starve on the high ground that had suddenly become islands. China's tragedy evoked the world's sympathy so that even Colonel Charles Lindbergh and his navigator wife flew to Nanking to help survey the watery desolation. Pearl was among those who greeted them; later at a dinner with Lossing, she met them again. With her usual forthrightness, she found Lindbergh to be "opinionated" but his wife "perfectly charming."

That same summer Absalom spent two happy months with Grace and her family in the mountains at Kuling. After years of hardship and privation, he was worn out and enjoyed the vacation. But in his weakened state, he contracted amoebic dysentery. Because of the flood, there was little anyone could do, and so Absalom's life came to an end. The high waters prevented Pearl from being with him, but she later made a pilgrimage to the mountain top where he was buried. "There is nothing between that spot and the sky, " she noted, "no tree, no human habitation. The rocks are beneath, the swirling mists about it."

As she stood by her father's lonely grave, no pious text came to her mind for comfort. Instead she recited the old Chinese proverb that seems to reflect so well the parent she had all her life tried so hard to understand:

The bright moon is not round for long,
The bright cloud is easily dispersed.

Furlough to America
~ CHAPTER 7

Political turmoil again beset China, for Chiang Kai-shek's pre-occupation with the Communists had left the country open to a Japanese attack. Things came to a climax in September, 1931, when Japan took over the city of Mukden in Manchuria. Although the Chinese leader appealed to the League of Nations in Geneva, the Japanese sent their gunboats up the Yangtse to Nanking.

In the early hours of a February morning, Pearl and her family awakened to a burst of heavy gunfire. Fortunately the guns in the Chinese fort did not respond, and no battle ensued. All American families again left the city.

The Bucks returned to Peking. Once they were settled, Pearl placed seven-year-old Janice in a day school. This freed her to explore the ancient city, making mental notes, as always, for future writings.

Meanwhile, Lloyd cabled the good news that MGM had offered fifty thousand dollars for the film rights to *The Good*

Earth. Pearl accepted. The book itself was still setting sales records and in seven months had gone through twelve printings. Cowboy actor and folk hero Will Rogers wrote in his syndicated newspaper column: "Don't tell me we have got people that can read and they haven't read Pearl Buck's great book on China, *The Good Earth.* It's not only the greatest book about a people ever written but the best book of our generation." People all across America rushed to get their own copy. In May, 1932, Pearl was awarded a Pulitzer Prize.

Lloyd also sold the dramatic rights of *The Good Earth.* Owen Davis would be the playwright, assisted by his son, Owen Davis, Jr., with Theater Guild producing. Such a prestigious combination of playwright and producer heralded a dramatic success.

About this time the Bucks returned to America so Lossing could get his Ph.D. at Cornell. Happily, they would be in Ithaca when the stage production of *The Good Earth* opened on the East Coast.

Prior to leaving China, Pearl decided that it was time for her father's translation of the New Testament into Chinese to be properly printed and bound. After accomplishing that task she packed her translation of *Shui Hu Chuan* into one huge suitcase for the journey to the U.S.

This time, they would sail to Vancouver, British Columbia, and take a train to Montreal. Richard drove to Montreal to meet them on July 19. Pearl had asked for as much privacy as was possible for their arrival, and whereas Richard Walsh respected this request, Pearl's brother Edgar unwittingly told the eager press all they wanted to know.

With the Bucks was Adeline Bucher, a cheerful young American who performed secretarial duties for Pearl and helped with Janice.

Miss Bucher was to take Janice to Lossing's parents' Pleasant Valley
farm, while Richard was to drive Pearl and Lossing to the Vermont
home of Lee Simonson, set designer for the Theater Guild. He
would then deliver them safely, if quietly, to the family farm.

This part of the plan worked smoothly, but on August 2,
1932, their lives changed drastically. They moved into a suite at
the Waldorf Astoria Hotel in New York City. There a press conference was arranged to save Pearl the strain of numerous individual interviews. The reporters were delighted to hear of Pearl's
reaction to receiving the Pulitzer Prize. Ishbel Ross would tell her
avid readers in the *New York Herald Tribune* the next day: "She
[Pearl] was dusting in the attic overlooking the pear trees in her
garden when a cable dispatch reached her that she had won the
Pulitzer Prize. She looked about for her husband. He wasn't in
the house, so she went on with her dusting."

Housewives across America loved it. Miss Ross also gave them
a glimpse of the famous author's husband, how he "sat beside his
wife as they talked, a slim figure with brown hair, smoked glasses
and a small reddish-blond moustache."

After the press conference, when Pearl and Lossing had rested,
they attended a dinner in the hotel's Jade Room to which the
elite of the literary world were invited. It was one of those hot
and humid August nights for which New York City is famous.
Yet even the dean of writers, Alexander Wolcott, left cool
Vermont to report on Pearl S. Buck. Upon arrival he was most
upset at being seated at a table reserved for Presbyterian missionaries instead of at the head table.

In his subsequent article in the *New Yorker* magazine,
Wolcott announced: "There, in Mrs. Buck's honor, on an

evening of unbearable heat, some two hundred-odd people assembled docilely and in a state of acute discomfort, stuffed themselves with expensive groceries, and then, in the ghastly tradition of such occasions, sat around on gold chairs and listened to speeches." But he also praised Pearl's humility when she revealed that throughout most of Chinese history, novelists were "ignored by their contemporaries."

The gregarious Lowell Thomas summed up the occasion perfectly when he told his radio audience, "World fame has come to this charming and exceedingly modest and soft-spoken American woman."

The time had also come for Pearl to clarify her position on the touchy subject of missionaries, with whom she had been involved all her life. Foreign mission boards across the country begged her to make a statement.

Pearl agreed to speak at what she thought would be a small luncheon, but to her chagrin she found it was to take place in the great ballroom at the Astor Hotel. There would be an audience of hundreds who would pay liberally for their tickets. For days she prepared her speech, which she was certain would upset some people, for she would not mince her words.

She said pointedly, "I can never have done with my apologies to the Chinese people that in the name of gentle Christ we have sent such people to them."

She proceeded to label some of the missionaries as arrogant, superstitious, ignorant, and downright cruel. One missionary, she declared, had seen fit to tell the ancestor-reverent Chinese that their forebears were all in hell.

Why, she wanted to know, did the mission boards so often send only their second best men and women in the service of the Lord? "The better ones often found themselves obliged to leave the service, so hampered by the criteria of membership rolls and statistics.... The missionary must go to fill a need, not to represent a creed."

"I am here," she continued, "speaking as one of you. By birth and ancestry I am an American, and by choice and belief I am a Christian, but by the years of my life, by sympathy and feeling, I am Chinese. So let me say to you what many Chinese have said to me, 'Come to us no more in arrogance of spirit. Come as brothers and fellow men. Let me see in you how your religion works. Preach to us no more, but share with us that better and more abundant life which your Christ lived. Give us your best or nothing.'"

There was dead silence in that great ballroom as Pearl S. Buck sat down.

Then the people began to clap, although mingled with their applause were cries of horror from the old guard. "It was appalling," Pearl later confessed. "It was as if I were alone in the middle of the Sahara."

Suddenly she saw Richard Walsh pushing his way through the desert of belligerent faces. Smiling, he squeezed her arm in reassurance. She had never felt so much in need of a friend in her life. He had been there when she most required support.

Richard later said, "It was your greatest moment; they should place a statue of you in the middle of Peking."

Certain Turmoil

⚜ CHAPTER 8

Richard Walsh suggested Pearl rest for two weeks following the uproar caused by her missionary speech. Even so, he told her of an intriguing invitation from Elmer Carter, editor of *Opportunity* magazine. She had been asked to tea with some prominent black women and himself in Harlem. Richard promised that he would investigate further, which he did, and reported that Elmer Carter thought a woman who could write so sympathetically as Pearl had done in *The Good Earth* was well worth knowing.

On December 11, 1932, accompanied by Richard, she kept the appointment, describing it as one of the most moving experiences of her entire life. The professional black women told Pearl how painful it was to be excluded from the mainstream of American life.

Later she attended an exhibition of paintings by black Americans and was deeply shocked by the subject matter: lynchings in the South, burned out slums and hungry children.

"What I saw, they had lived," Pearl declared, "prejudice and segregation and denial of opportunity."

Throughout her Chinese childhood, Carie had instilled in her eldest daughter the memories of an America that was heaven on earth. Pearl was shattered by the rude awakening and vowed to read everything she could about America's black population. If she ever returned to America for good, they would be her first concern. For the present she could at least write some articles for Elmer Carter's magazine.

Speaking before a predominantly black audience at the New School for Social Research in New York City, Pearl called herself black for the day, and noted: "We are not foreigners here. We are Americans, but sometimes we are afraid we are not really as good as the white man because we cannot forget our fathers were slaves…we can never become accustomed to the slights…we must equally believe in each other, to keep up our morale."

In the midst of such a busy life, Pearl did not forget Carol. She presented a generous check for $50,000 to Dr. Johnstone, some of which was to be used to build the Carol Cottage in which her daughter would live with other girls and a housemother. It would have its own wading pool and playground. The rest of the gift was to be used for research to help other similarly afflicted children.

In spite of her problems, Carol surprisingly had a gift for enjoying good music. She would listen to records of a symphony for hours at a time, actually crying when the music seemed very sad.

Janice was sometimes quietly brought to visit her sister by Miss Bucher. With the kidnapping of the Lindbergh baby still fresh in people's minds, Pearl was very fearful that her own children might suffer the same fate. To ease her worries, Ruby Walsh, Richard's wife, often invited Janice to stay with her while Pearl travelled to speaking engagements.

On April 18, 1933, Pearl was unpleasantly shocked by a call from a *New York Post* reporter. He phoned to ask if it were true that she was to be tried by her church on a charge of heresy unless she made it clear that the Chinese born before the arrival of foreign missionaries were condemned to eternal damnation.

Asking the reporter to call back, she contacted Richard Walsh and requested that he look into the matter at once. It appeared that the Reverend J. Gresham Machen, a professor with the Westminster Theological Assembly in Philadelphia, was responsible. Dr. Machen suggested that not only should she be tried for heresy but that every member of the mission board should be dismissed. He was infuriated by Pearl's article in *Harper's* magazine entitled, "Is There a Case for Foreign Missions?" together with another in *Cosmopolitan*. In the latter, Dr. Machen had taken exception to Pearl's statement that "except in places of formal worship, one seldom hears Christ's name and there He is not to be found for me."

For two weeks the New York tabloids had a field day. In the end, a statement she had written with Richard's help was given to the eager reporters. It declared: "I shall not make a martyr of myself, nor shall I engage in any controversy to justify my position. I shall hold to the article in *Harper's* for my credo on missions, and I cannot explain it away. No notice has been given me of any impending action and I have nothing further to say."

With Richard as intermediary, Pearl was able to resign with dignity from what she called her "active connection with the Presbyterian Board of Foreign Missions." It was emphasized that Lossing would still retain his position with the Mission.

Her decision certainly did not trouble Yale University, which in June bestowed on her an honorary Master of Arts degree. At the ceremony, William Lyons Phelps, Dean of English, called her "the ablest living interpreter of the Chinese character," adding, "In view of Yale's long and close affiliation with China, it is especially fitting that she should become one of us."

Equally pleasing was the commencement speech Pearl was asked to give at her own Randolph-Macon Woman's College. She was fashionably dressed this time, unlike the day she had first arrived as a student, attired so differently from the other girls. Emma Edmunds White, her one friend that lonely day, was again on hand, this time to witness Pearl's triumph.

Pearl attended all the rehearsals she could manage of the stage adaptation of *The Good Earth*. She was absolutely mesmerized by the theater. The play was to open first in Philadelphia with Alla Nazimova as O-lan and an actor named Larrimore as Wang Lung.*

With so much other activity, work was going slowly on *The Mother*, the third novel in the trilogy of which *The Good Earth* was the first and *Sons* the second. In *The Mother*, one of her most memorable novels, she tells the story of a woman abandoned by

---

* Alla Nazimova, one of the greatest dramatic actresses of her generation, was godmother of a girl who in later life as Nancy Reagan would become First Lady of the United States of America. Nancy's mother, Edith Luckett, was a friend and fellow actress of the Russian star.

her husband, son and daughter-in-law. Although she is burdened   83
with a blind daughter, she nevertheless makes ends meet. It is
somewhat reminiscent of the Biblical story of the widow's mite.

Pearl decided to stay in Ithaca and write while Richard Walsh
attended the tryout in Philadelphia. He later reported that while
Nazimova was "extraordinary," Larrimore and Henry Travers
were not. The play was in need of work. Claude Rains was asked
to replace Larrimore. Then, after what seemed an eternity to
Pearl, the play opened November 14 at the Guild Theater in
New York.

It was lambasted by most of the critics. The powerful Brooks
Atkinson proclaimed that "in the exact proportion that *The Good
Earth* is a good and excellent novel, it is an empty play."
Nazimova, though praised in the early scenes, was panned in the
others when, according to Atkinson, "Her acting subsides into
tortuous grimaces and her speaking becomes a series of primor-
dial sounds."

Richard told Pearl not to upset herself. It was the play that had
failed, not her original novel. Besides, he had better news to dwell
on. *Sons,* the story of Wang Lung's greedy offspring, had an enormous advance sale.

Another year expired and it was time to return to their
home in China. Pearl wanted to show appreciation to her in-laws
so she paid off the mortgage on the family farm. She gave them a
radio, had shrubbery planted in their yard, built them a porch
and enlarged their living room. Then she had the portrait she had
commissioned of herself hung over the mantelpiece. Pearl gave
the senior Bucks and her husband Lossing annuities amounting

to five thousand dollars each. She had a new chimney built on her brother-in-law Clifford's house and the structure itself painted white and hung with green shutters.

The return to China would be the reverse of the European trip Pearl had experienced as a child. Prior to departure, she visited Carol at the training school and accompanied Lossing to Cornell University, where he was awarded his Ph.D. With Janice and Miss Bucher, they later joined Richard and Ruby Walsh on the *Empress of Britain* and steamed for Liverpool.

Once in Britain, Miss Bucher and Janice were given their own London flat while Pearl and Lossing explored the countryside by car. Lossing and Ardron Lewis, who was to help him with the land utilization work in China, then toured another three weeks, during which Pearl went to Sweden with the Walshes. At summer's end, the Walshes sailed home. Lossing, Pearl, Lewis, Miss Bucher and Janice continued on by car to Venice.

It was in Nice that Carie's long-ago prediction about Pearl's marriage came true. Lossing's preoccupation with his agricultural work had left Pearl feeling neglected for some time and she had naturally been drawn to Richard Walsh, with whom she had much more in common. She had fallen in love with him and, apparently, he felt equally attracted to her. When Pearl suddenly asked Lossing for a separation, he seemed prepared for it. Although she accompanied him on to China, their marriage was essentially over.

Marriage to Richard Walsh

✦ CHAPTER 9

The Great Depression was in full force and back in New York, Richard Walsh, like many other Americans, was having financial problems at the John Day Company. To help his situation he took on the additional responsibilities of editing *Asia* magazine, the first publication in the United States to accept Pearl's articles.*

To help Richard's cash flow, Pearl reduced her royalty payments by purchasing 300 copies of *All Men Are Brothers,* her translation of *Shui Hu Chuan*. In addition, advance sales for *The Mother* were "perfectly extraordinary" and with the filming of *The Good Earth* and expected sales increases in the book itself, Richard was optimistic that his financial troubles would soon be over. With great confidence, he planned a trip to China to take photographs for the magazine. He would

* The publishers of *Asia* magazine were Leonard Elmhurst and his wife, Dorothy Whitney Elmhurst, the widow of Willard Straight. Straight had founded the magazine after being a U.S. Consul in Peking.

leave his assistant, Critchell Rimington, in charge of the John Day office.

Pearl was elated when she heard that Richard was coming. She had promised to have a new book written to coincide with her publisher's arrival, but with her marriage in shambles she had been so unhappy that, instead of writing, she had spent her time working in the garden.

Lossing, on the other hand, had no need nor desire to see Richard Walsh. Just prior to Walsh's arrival, Lossing left for Tibet with a group of soil specialists. His marriage had always been secondary to his career, so he immersed himself in his work. Although Pearl could see no future for herself in China, Lossing's was bright.

Richard duly arrived with his new Leica camera and was immediately whisked off by Pearl to visit her sister Grace. The Yaukeys' third child, Anne, had been born a hopeless invalid. Pearl sadly realized that it was Carol all over again and felt a great need to comfort her sister and provide whatever assistance to the family she could.

From Grace's home, Pearl and Richard continued their travels, visiting Indo-China and India in the company of other writers and editors, and then returned to Peking. There, Pearl presented Richard to Lin Yutang, a political essayist. Lin in turn introduced the New York publisher to two other writers living just outside Peking, Edgar Snow and his wife, Helen Foster Snow. Mrs. Snow found it strange for a sophisticated man like Richard Walsh "to be mixed up with a missionary." However, the Snows spent a most enjoyable day entertaining Pearl and Richard, who, they decided, were happy and productive in their endeavors together.

Richard's photography assignment then took him on to
Manchuria. Pearl stayed to visit doctors at the University of
Peking Medical College for advice as to how she could best help
her little niece, Anne.

On May 30, 1934, with Janice and Miss Bucher, Pearl joined
Richard once again and boarded the steamship *Empress of
Russia,* bound for Canada. While the voyage was pleasant, the
arrival in Vancouver was not, for Critchell Rimington was wait-
ing for Richard with the startling news that the John Day
Company was bankrupt.

Almost immediately they faced a second calamity. Due to a
malfunction in the new camera, every photograph Richard had
taken on his travels was blank.

Richard Walsh refused to admit defeat. Back in New
York, he fought to save the business. He released his staff, with
the exception of his secretary, mortgaged his home, borrowed
money on his life insurance, and got his printers to agree to
accept stock in lieu of cash.

Pearl had moved into a penthouse apartment overlooking the
East River. She sent Janice to a summer camp near her in-laws'
farm, then proceeded to help Richard bail out of his difficulties.
She told him to withhold her sizeable royalties and offered to
take an advisory editor's job with his firm. Encouraged by her
presence, literary agents again submitted manuscripts. Then the
publishers, Reynal and Hitchcock, agreed to promote, produce
and distribute books by the John Day Company. In time, much
to his own personal satisfaction, Richard Walsh paid off every
cent owed by the business.

One day, while sitting in her new office, Pearl recalled the cardboard box containing the manuscript about Carie, her mother. She had never intended it for publication, but when Richard read it, he was delighted. They titled it *The Exile,* and Richard decided it would be the John Day offering for January, 1936. The *Woman's Home Companion* paid Pearl $25,000 for the condensation rights. She immediately loaned the money to Richard's company.

Satisfied that she could now attend to more personal matters, Pearl again focused on her family. She was relieved to hear that Grace and Jesse were leaving the dangerous part of China, which had become a warlords' battleground, and were bringing their children to America. Pearl planned the best treatment possible for their daughter Anne as soon as the Yaukey family arrived in the United States.

She was also determined to write a play of her own, an obsession that would plague her for the rest of her life. In spite of the sad fate of the stage adaptation of *The Good Earth,* she was still fascinated by the theater, and took in every Broadway play she could.

She began to write her play in the summer of 1934. The finished effort took the prestigious Theater Guild only ten days to reject. Deciding that one day she would pen a better play, Pearl went back to her other writings and soon sold a novelette to *Cosmopolitan* magazine.

She also found time to search for and find the house of her dreams, which she bought for $4,100. She made the down payment before leaving the property, for it was love at first sight.

Located not far from Carol's Vineland School in New Jersey,

the forty-eight acre property included an ancient stone farmhouse
that had been empty for seventeen years. It also had a garden
choked with thorns and weeds. Janice, who was about to attend
Brearley School in New York City, loved it. In the years to come,
Pearl would spend thousands of dollars to restore both the house
and the land to their former productive beauty. She would call
her new abode Green Hills Farm.

Pearl suggested to her brother Edgar that he live in a small
stone house close by. She was deeply concerned about his health
as well, for he had a troubling heart problem. In spite of that
affliction, Edgar had done well. He had remarried and his
American population studies and research as an economist had
brought him much recognition and thus had the honor of
becoming the Public Health Service's first statistician.

In the fall, the sculptor Malvina Hoffman sublet her
house in Murray Hill, New York City, to Pearl. This was closer to
her work, and here, Richard could visit frequently. He treated her
delightfully, and made her laugh when she tried to be serious. She
was thoroughly enjoying life in America and the thought of
returning to China became more repugnant.

Richard soon proposed that they divorce their respective
spouses and marry, but there was still a certain stigma to divorce,
and she knew the public was fickle. Would her thousands of
women readers accept a divorce from a missionary husband and a
new marriage to her publisher? She decided to take the risk.

At the invitation of the Treasury Department, Lossing arrived
that October to advise on its plan to purchase much of China's
silver, for his report entitled "Silver and Prices in China" had won

much praise. Pearl went to the Treasury to ask him for a divorce, and was somewhat taken aback to find that her soon-to-be-former husband had been given such a fine office.

Lossing immediately agreed to her wishes, and one of the last acts Pearl performed as his wife was to deed the farm in Pleasant Valley to her in-laws for life. In kindness, she did not interfere with the annuities that she had bestowed on the elderly couple.

As divorces go, this one was, to say the least, unconventional. Pearl and Ruby Walsh both left for Reno, Nevada, to establish legal residence before their respective divorces. After waiting out the necessary six weeks, on June 11, 1935, their separate suits were heard before Judge Thomas F. Moran. Ruby Walsh charged her husband with cruelty, and her divorce was granted in five minutes. She was awarded alimony of $4,800 a year, which she had agreed to on May 6.

Pearl's suit, charging Lossing with incompatibility, took longer—fifteen minutes. She asked her former husband for nothing, giving him the furniture in both the Chinese home and that which she owned in his family name. The *New York News* headlines read "DIVORCE WITHOUT PASSION."

While Ruby left the court by a rear door, Pearl chose the main entrance where Richard Walsh was waiting. Shortly afterwards, they were married by the Reverend R. C. Thompson, Dean of Men at the University of Nevada. The bride wore a white dress, a blue cape and a straw hat. They drove to Lake Tahoe for their honeymoon.

Asia *Magazine Book Shelf*

CHAPTER 10

The bridal couple returned to New York, unprepared for the furor over their marriage. Besieged by reporters, they finally took refuge in the farmhouse that Pearl had bought in the country. Little peace could be found there either, for the curious came down their private road just to look in the windows. Pearl finally had the road closed and later removed altogether. In spite of all this Pearl could still write, "I am really happy, it seems to me, for the first time in my life, and so I am at peace."

As was to have been expected, missionary spokesmen were rabid in their criticism of the marriage, especially those from the South. Pearl felt that the only honorable thing was to offer her withdrawal from a scheduled appearance at the Virginia University Institute of Public Affairs. However, the university was adamant that she should speak, declaring, "This is an Institute of Public Affairs, not of private affairs."

So, with Richard to give her moral support, the new Mrs. Walsh lectured to a full house on the differences between Chinese and

Americans. In her opinion, the Chinese, free of the puritanical influences of the American forefathers, seem to have come off the better. "And while the sense of sin is typical of the Puritanic residue," she hammered home, "the Chinese, born without it, lives in tune with his environment, afflicted with no sense of inborn personal unworthiness conflicting with his natural influences."

Pearl entered into this new phase of her life with zest and enthusiasm. Both her energy and her interests seemed limitless.

In March 1935, *Asia* magazine, now owned by Richard Walsh, announced that Pearl S. Buck would be the new editor of its book review section, "Book Shelf." In addition to editing all reviews submitted for this section, she read voraciously, writing her monthly reviews with the same ease that she continued to turn out her novels. In addition, during this same period she gave freely of her knowledge of Asian life, helping to insure the authenticity of such works as the popular novel *Anna and the King of Siam.*

In the first months, she wrote in her column of rapidly changing conditions in the world. "Change is the atmosphere of our generation and change has us all in its cyclonic grasp. Even the shape of the future is not as important as the fact of our present universal movement and struggle."

Referring to the worldwide depression, she wrote: "Never before has the world been so unified by similar experience as it is now. Every country is involved in change, and it may be that this similarity may do more toward final international understanding than any treaty. And the experience is not, I think, important only because it is national and international, but because individuals everywhere are facing the same need to find ground of some

sort under their feet, to be secure in some place and group. It is   **93**
the common need of the modern soul."

In succeeding years, her reviews included such wide-ranging
subjects as art, music and flower arrangement. She said, "If there
be too many travel books about Asia, there can never be enough
on the art, science, education and sociology of Asia.... Most
regretfully there is not enough yet being written by Asians."
Richard agreed with her, publishing such famous Asiatic writers
as Jawaharlal Nehru, Carlos Romulo, Hu Shih, and Pahk Induk.

In her review of *Men and Ideas* by Lin Mousheng she wrote:
"The Chinese are the most modern minded of all the peoples of
Asia not because they are westernized in the usual sense of the
word but because they have kept through the centuries a mind so
fluid, so unbound by social and political traditions that they have
been ready at all times for change. So they are ready mentally and
spiritually even for this strange day in which we live.

"The Chinese demanded of their thinkers practical values.
These were essentially moral values but the Chinese wisely believe
that moral values pay a good deal more than their price in direct
returns of peace and prosperity. Goodwill among men is valuable
not as a religious asset but as an excellent atmosphere for trade. A
good man as emperor was the best surety for good government.
Good citizens insured good business. Tyranny in the palace and
crime in the street merely made life a nuisance for all concerned.
For above all else the Chinese love life, its pleasures, its work and
play. Virtue, they reasoned, made for the abundant life not in
heaven but on earth. Therefore they told their thinkers, 'teach us
all high and low, what is the superior man, not for some future
state but here and now.'

"With such demands it was impossible for the Chinese to retreat into abstractions. The people held them grimly to earth and made them think to the point of practical need....

"Here is modern thinking not ancient. The road which we travel, the road which we think is so new has been travelled before by Chinese feet. Perhaps that is why China meets her present disaster with such unyielding courage and such unpuzzled calm. She has lived through a flurry of lesser men before in her own history and has come through to freedom and the realities of her own life and so she shall again. Such courage and such calm ought to be a tower of strength to us now and a foundation of wisdom to us at the peace table, when tangled relations must be untangled.

"There is another reason I am glad to introduce this book. The author not only reveals the thinkers who have shaped the thoughts of the Chinese but he reveals most interesting and significant parallels to western philosophical thinking. Our philosophers, East and West, in the span of history though unknowingly and at different times have thought alike. Human beings are human beings still. We need today to have practical proof of our likeness to each other and here it is. Not only is there nothing alien to us now in Chinese thought but actually our thinkers have done the same sort of thinking.... Our differences in thought have been superficial and our likenesses profound. It is time we knew it."

Her reviews for the "Book Shelf" give her readers insight into Pearl's thoughts and interests. She, like her mother, continued to search for a deeper meaning in life.

In reviewing Daniel Fleming's *Each with his Own Brush,* she remarked, "Artists see the inner human beauty of old legends and that understanding is the more precious and rare when it is without particular religious belief." Comments like these had earned her a reputation for being irreligious, but this was far from the truth. She dreamed of a more perfect understanding of religion, broader than the narrow concepts of her day, and she felt that many others were searching even as she was.

When reviewing a book on mysticism, she observed, "The book is timely because everywhere in the world there is a reviving interest in the subject, a phenomenon common enough in history in times of stress and uncertainty."

In her review of four books on Hinduism and Buddhism she commented: "One hundred years from now historians will see this period (in all its confusion) as an awakening of interest in the religions of the Orient.... It is important that the 'awakening' will not be reactionary but rather a sincere search for what has most helped, comforted and stimulated the human soul everywhere."

This was in contrast with her review of a book which was billed as a religious book. "Good travel book but there is little knowledge or evidence [of religious understanding] in *Tibetan Buddhism,* which can be profoundly philosophical. One feels religion was a pretext to enter the country which does not welcome visitors."

The importance of history was a constantly recurring theme. She wrote: "It is an absurdity that 4,000 years of living by a quarter of the human race has been crowded into a few pages. Which, more often than not, gives no emphasis to matters of real importance in Chinese history. The cause? Simple ignorance. Even eminent western historians have been too ignorant to value properly the importance of Chinese history in its relation to all of human history."

She expressed her romantic nature in a review of *Plant Hunter's Paradise* by F. Kingdon Ward. "Once in a while, a book comes along which is entirely different from any other. It is passionately written by someone who passionately pursues a single idea and through the lens of that idea, vocation or hobby one sees the world from a new point of view.... This is such a book. It makes one realize afresh that ALL the world is not involved by man in its destruction—there is a world where birds sing, rare flowers grow on strange unknown slopes and animals pursue their ways. It is well to remember that."

She used her boundless energy to promote respect for the Asian mind, philosophy and way of life as a viable alternative to the customs of the western world. She wanted our scholars to appreciate the monumental endeavor involved in Nehru's *Glimpses of World History,* which he wrote in prison without a single note from any textbook or research materials. She saw a danger in foreign students coming to America for their education and not returning to enrich their native lands by their knowledge. "Foreign students must in the main go back to their people and take that which they have learned abroad and be a part of their own people's struggle." Regarding a reporter's book on Asia, she wrote: "Here is an orgy of romance, adventure and excitement. It is all very interesting with 'scoop' after 'scoop'. But one soon senses how ephemeral and unrealistic it all is let alone shallow and not rooted in history."

She emphasized that the truest picture of other peoples came from those people themselves, not from some outsider, who, after a brief visit, considered himself an expert on the nation he had visited. In the review of a book by two Americans hopping about

Asia, she commented: "I used to see Americans like these two
knocking about in China. They went home and wrote what they
thought was amusing in their books. But their books were no
more delightful than the long-chuckling reminiscences of the
Chinese after they had gone back to America. The absurdities of
the strangers' customs, their exasperating traits and extraordinary
ignorance of good behavior were remembered and discussed,
roared at with laughter and gravely regretted."

During the height of *Asia* magazine's popularity, Pearl was
increasingly concerned that lack of understanding of other cultures and other ways of thinking were leading the Western world
into armed conflict with the Eastern countries. Regarding the
Sino-Japanese War in 1936 she warned: "There may come some
day in the far far distant future when such minds shall be judged
as insane and unfit for human freedom. Only then will the rest of
us be safe and ourselves be free to live."

World War II was becoming a frightening possibility, and Pearl
felt that the United States' foreign policy was not adequate to
prevent it. A. W. Griswold's book, *Far East Policy of the United
States*, fostered her fears. "The book presents a dismaying picture
of which every intelligent American must be ashamed. A picture
of utmost confusion. No surrealist could paint a more illogical
display. There is a lack of continuity of policy. Policies are formed
on the exigency of some moment. Policies are not understood
and seldom foreseen. There is incredible ineptitude."

By the end of World War II there was little improvement, and
she commented: "I wish this book could be put on every
American doorstep tomorrow morning along with the daily
newspaper and the milk bottle. Revered names quiver as the

author quotes their own words and their own absurd mistakes."

During World War II news from Asia became scarce, causing the Walshes to change the title and purpose of *Asia* magazine to *Asia and the Americas*. When the war was over, the burgeoning of new periodicals caused them to merge with the magazine known as *United Nations World*.

If Pearl felt more secure in her own home life, so did her daughter Janice. Janice was a very compassionate child and genuinely fond of Carol. She had stayed near Carol's training school while their mother was in Nevada getting the divorce. Now, her mother told her, "Uncle Dick" could be called "Daddy."

In January, 1936, Carie's story, *The Exile,* was well received, both by the critics and Pearl's readers. The Book-of-the-Month Club chose it and the story of her father, *Fighting Angel,* as a joint offering.*

Pearl, who was busy making extensive and expensive renovations to her farm house, as well as paying for her niece Anne's medical expenses, considered this latest honor to be "the best thing that could happen to me both professionally and financially." *The Exile* had actually been reviewed on the front of the all important *New York Times Book Review,* which called her efforts "a richly human record." *Fighting Angel* merited pride of place in another issue of the same magazine, saying Pearl "had touched problems as deep as all humanity."

But *Fighting Angel* also made Pearl once again the target of her former fellow missionaries' wrath. This time they accused her of "unchristianly behavior." Angrily she responded, "I have no

* In *Fighting Angel,* Pearl changed Absalom's given name to Andrew.

patience with nonsense like the anger of a few missionaries over what I wrote of my own parents." Like father, like daughter. Old Absalom would have reacted likewise.

Richard's children by his first marriage and his mother seem to have accepted Pearl into their orbit, for they joined them for Christmas dinner in New York. The day before, with Richard, she had visited Carol, who seemed better than her mother could ever remember. The wretched spasms with which she had been afflicted had disappeared.

Richard was very supportive of his new wife over her retarded daughter. Carol, he felt, "might have been his own child." Because he had a wonderful way with all children, she responded quickly to his friendliness.

However, he longed for children of his own with Pearl and she with him, but as she could bear no others, adoption was the only solution. First they talked it over with Janice, who welcomed the idea. Through the reputable organization in Chicago known as the Cradle, they became parents in February, 1936, of two month-old baby boys, born two days apart. These were duly named John Stulting Walsh and Richard Stulting Walsh.

For the first few weeks Pearl and Richard were real parents and took complete charge of the new arrivals, although to Pearl's amusement Richard drew the line at changing diapers. In their commute between their new apartment at 480 Park Avenue, New York City, and Green Hills Farm, the Walshes used large market baskets in lieu of cradles for the babies. En route, Richard thought nothing of marching into a Howard Johnson's restaurant to have the milk bottles warmed.

The following year they adopted two other little ones, Edgar and Jean. Miss Kaye, a registered nurse, was engaged to help. And when guests came, regardless of their relative importance in society and the world, Miss Kaye was summoned with the children so that Pearl could show off her babies. Janice, now tall as her mother, had developed an early maternal feeling for the four infants. She helped Nurse Kaye feed and bathe them and enjoyed every minute of it.

In March of 1936, Pearl's brother Edgar died. They had grown close again after he had moved near the farm. He was wonderful with the babies and she was reminded of him as he used to be in their Chinese childhood, the elder brother who took his two-year-old sister by the hand through the sweet, old-fashioned rose garden. Edgar had refused to see a doctor, saying that he was too busy. Now he was gone.

The Yaukeys had settled with their little family in Fall River, Massachusetts. With Pearl's encouragement, Grace was doing some writing of her own, using the pen name Cornelia Spencer. She was a devoted mother to little Anne who, in spite of all the medical attention her aunt had provided, never got any better. The child finally died.

On February 2, 1937, the motion picture *The Good Earth* opened with much fanfare in New York. Unlike the book, it climaxed with a plague of locusts, a change that Pearl had approved. Reviewers likened the tale to the Biblical stories Pearl had been taught in her youth. She wished that a Chinese might have played the peasant hero, Wang Lung, for in spite of all the makeup and fine acting, Paul Muni remained essentially American. However, the part of Wang Lung's

Rare photo of Mr. and Mrs. Walsh with Janice and four of their adopted children taken in front of Pearl's birthplace at Hillsboro, West Virginia.

longsuffering wife, O-Lan, was played with such perfection by Luise Rainer that perhaps, Pearl remarked, she really was Chinese. Miss Rainer won her second Oscar for the brilliant portrayal. Proud and happy, Pearl watched the premiere from a seat in the gallery, then and there deciding that she had one challenge left. She still had to write a successful play.

She would call her play *The Empress*. Tz'u Hsi, the Chinese ruler of her own childhood, would be the heroine. After a period of intense labor, Pearl offered the completed work to the great Katherine Cornell, whom she had seen play a Malaysian princess on stage in *The Winged Victory*.

Miss Cornell said she would be happy to read Pearl's play, for China's last Empress had always fascinated her. She would then show it to her husband, director-producer Guthrie McClintic.

Although the Walshes and McClintics visited each others' homes, the relationship was far from satisfactory and it was further strained as Pearl waited for Cornell's decision. Cornell insisted that she loved the play, but her husband suggested changes, which Pearl produced in record time.

Yet, Cornell procrastinated. She was tired after the long run in *The Winged Victory*, and besides, she wondered if it would be wise to play another Asian woman so soon. Still, she had always been intrigued by "Old Buddha," as she called Ts'u Hzi. Finally, when told by Pearl that another famous theatrical couple, Alfred Lunt and Lynn Fontanne, were hunting for a play set in China, Cornell responded that perhaps the Lunts should have it. She could not consider *The Empress* for another eighteen months.

Despite Cornell's reaction to *The Empress*, Pearl decided to send the McClintics her other work, *Flight into China*. Completion of both plays was announced in the press, but somehow, contracts never **103** materialized.

Undaunted, Pearl sent them *The Crystal Heart,* a third play that offered a contemporary setting. But Cornell's and Pearl's interpretation of the modern woman were not on the same plane. Cornell insisted, "The modern woman that I want to play must have a great universal theme."

Pearl countered, "I have not as yet seen any modern woman whom I consider great, and for the present at least I don't see a play about a great modern woman."

In the meantime, Pearl asked Cornell if she would mind if *The Empress* were offered to someone else since Pearl was writing other plays for her. Again Cornell was noncommittal. In desperation Pearl asked Helen Hayes to take the role. Not knowing of Cornell's involvement, Miss Hayes, who recognized herself as a most unlikely candidate for the role, tactfully suggested that they "try Katherine Cornell" for "the role cries out for her."

Then the actress, playwright, novelist and poet Mary Kennedy came into the picture. As chairman of the drama committee for the prestigious Cosmopolitan Club, she suggested a reading of *The Empress* for the club's membership. As Pearl had designated ten sets and a cast of fifty-one in addition to extras, Miss Kennedy knew *The Empress* had to be cut in order to be workable—but first there had to be a preliminary reading with those who would play the leading roles. Cornelia Otis Skinner would be the Empress, Vincent Price her unlikely lover. Others in the cast included Jane Wyatt and Margalo Gillmore. It took all of four hours to read through their parts, and they were exhausted. Afterwards Miss Skinner and Miss Gillmore literally got out their pencils and reduced the script to a more suitable length.

On the night of the performance, wearing embroidered coats that Miss Kennedy had found in China, the principals sat at little tables to give their reading before the club ladies and several of their husbands. There was a shortage of scripts, so Price and Skinner had to share one. As she later good-naturedly complained, "One of us being quite short-sighted and the other very long, we had to keep the script politely seesawing back and forth to each other's sight level."

Pearl, a fellow member, sat in the front row center, her face expressionless, horrified at the way her play had been cut. Two weeks later she curtly wrote the leading lady:

> Dear Miss Skinner:
>
> Thank you very much for taking part in the reading of my play *The Empress* at the Cosmopolitan Club.
>
> Sincerely,
>
> Pearl S. Buck

Ten years afterwards, Mary Kennedy described the reading in a *New Yorker* magazine article aptly entitled, "Actors Will Do Anything."

Even after all this, *The Empress* refused to die. To appease his wife's hurt feelings, Richard sent the uncut version to Myron Selznick, the West Coast theatrical agent, to see if it contained any motion picture potential. Of the ill-fated play, Selznick observed: "It is good *reading* writing. That is, it is well written but doesn't seem to have the possibilities to play. You might tell Mrs. Buck [sic] that this is the fault most novelists have when they turn to playwriting—their plays just refuse to play."

November 10, 1937 was gray and foreboding. Pearl had breakfasted as usual with Richard; then, still in her favorite old blue velvet robe, she disappeared into her writing room to work. Suddenly she was interrupted by an excited Miss Bucher with somewhat startling news. "You've won the Nobel Prize!"

"I can't believe it!" Pearl exclaimed. "That's ridiculous. The report must be a mistake."

After Richard called her Swedish publisher to confirm the news, she dressed quickly and hurried to the John Day office to meet with the press. "It should have gone to Theodore Dreiser," she somewhat humbly noted. When asked how she would spend the prize money, Pearl jokingly reminded the reporters that she would now have to pay extra taxes. Richard, good public relations man that he was, handled the publicity personally. The next morning, the nation's newspapers praised Pearl for being the first

American woman to win the Nobel Prize for Literature. During the month before the actual presentation, Pearl was feted at a dinner given by P.E.N., the writers' association, after which the novelist Sinclair Lewis, a previous winner, had a few private words of advice to render. Ever after, he declared, people would discuss her first great success, *The Good Earth,* as if it were the only book she had ever written, as they had done with his *Main Street.* She would become sick and tired of hearing about *The Good Earth,* but she must "let people have their little say for they have nothing else to say." He advised her to enjoy her moment of triumph as the greatest in her life as a writer.

Pearl never forgot Lewis's words. Later, on learning of his lonely death in Italy, she wrote: "I had supposed a man so famous and so successful would have been surrounded by old and faithful friends. I had heard of his faults and difficulties but his genius was a burden heavy enough for him to bear, and because of it, surely he should have been forgiven by his friends."

On a visit to Lewis's old home at Sauk Centre, Minnesota, she declared, "I could see him bursting out of these walls, out of the town and what it stood for, loving it so much that he hated it for not being all he wanted it to be, and knew it could be."

Several other writers were not so generous to their feminine contemporary as Sinclair Lewis had been. For a Southerner, William Faulkner was downright unchivalrous, commenting of the Nobel Prize, "I don't want it. I'd rather be in the company of Sherwood Anderson and Theodore Dreiser than S. Lewis and Mrs. 'Chinahand' Buck." The poet Robert Frost was equally nasty, snarling, "If she can get it, anybody can."

Sweden's Selma Lagerlöf informed Pearl that her vote was

based upon the biographies of Pearl's parents that she had so sympathetically written and not just for *The Good Earth*. This view was substantiated by Anders Osterling, Permanent Secretary of the Swedish Academy and Chairman of the Nobel Committee on Literature. He explained that the Academy's decision to award her the coveted prize "was, above all, for the admirable biographies of her parents, the missionary pair in China, two volumes that seemed to deserve classic rank and to possess the required prospects for permanent interest. In addition, other novels of Chinese peasant life have properly made a place for themselves by virtue of the authority, wealth of detail and rare insight with which they describe a region that is little known and rarely accessible to Western readers. But as literary works of art the two biographies remain incomparable with anything else in Pearl Buck's earlier or later production."

Meanwhile, all was hustle and bustle in the Walsh homes as Pearl prepared for her trip to Sweden. She bought five evening gowns with trains to match, together with several pairs of the traditional long white gloves. Miss Kaye, the efficient governess, and Mrs. Loris, the cook, were to care for the household affairs. Richard carefully packed the traditional white tie and tails, while his daughter Betty, excited at having her first evening gown, was pleased to accompany them to Sweden.

They arrived in Stockholm in midwinter. Pearl, along with Enrico Fermi, the Italian physicist and also a Nobel Prize recipient, were overwhelmed with attention. She was assigned a personal attaché to help her through the royal protocol of the actual ceremony. She was also shown how to properly curtsy before the

King and then walk backwards to her seat without tripping, no easy feat for a woman with a train! At the appropriate time she accomplished both successfully and was given a thunderous ovation by the audience.

Pearl's and Fermi's arrival in the great hall was announced by trumpets, which in that ancient place sounded almost medieval. The King, together with other members of the Royal Family and Academy members, all in formal dress, faced them from a platform. Separate speeches in Swedish, of which both recipients had seen translations beforehand, lauded their accomplishments. They each received citations, a gold medal and a check. All of Pearl's books were mentioned in the citation with the exception of her latest, *This Proud Heart,* which had been published too late to be included.

Over a thousand guests attended the dinner afterward in the Gold Room. Pearl was placed between the Crown Prince and his son, while King Gustaf and two princesses sat opposite.

Pearl's acceptance speech particularly impressed the Swedes.

> Your Royal Highnesses:
>
> Ladies and Gentlemen:
>
> It is not possible for me to express all that I feel of appreciation for what has been said and given to me. I accept, for myself, with the conviction of having received far beyond what I have been able to give in my books. I can only hope that the many books which I have yet to write will be in some measure a worthier acknowledgement than I can make tonight. And indeed, I can accept only in the same spirit in which I think this gift was originally given—that it is a prize not so much for what has been done as for the future. Whatever I write in the future

Nobel Prize for Literature being presented to Pearl Buck by the King of Sweden.

must, I think, be always benefitted and strengthened when I remember this day.

I accept, too, for my country, the United States of America. We are a people still young, and we know we have not yet come to the fullness of our powers. This award, given to an American, strengthens not only one, but the whole body of American writers, who are encouraged and heartened by such generous recognition. And I should like to say, too, that in my country it is important that this award has been given to a woman. You who have already so recognized your own Selma Lagerlöf, and have long recognized women in other fields, cannot perhaps wholly understand what it means in many countries that it is a woman who stands here at this moment. But I speak not only for writers and for women, but for all Americans, for we all share in this.

I should not be truly myself if I did not, in my own wholly unofficial way, speak also of the people of China, whose life has for so many years been my life also, whose life, indeed, must always be a part of my life. The minds of my own country and of China, my foster country, are alike in many ways, but above all, in our common love of freedom. And today more than ever, this is true, now when China's whole being is engaged in the greatest of all struggles, the struggle for freedom. I have never admired China more than I do now, when I see her uniting as she has never done before, against the enemy who threatens her freedom. With this determination for freedom, which is in so profound a sense the essential quality in her nature, I know that she is *unconquerable*. Freedom—it is today more than ever the most precious human possession. We—Sweden and the United States—we have it still. My country is young—but it greets you with a peculiar fellowship, you whose earth is ancient and free.

In a few words Pearl S. Buck had forcefully represented women's rights and freedom of the individual. Sadly, only China's own Nationalist representative chose to stay away from the ceremony at the last minute, miffed by an interview on China's future that Pearl had given in Denmark en route to the awards. In it she had emphasized that a strong central government was China's one solution to peace, that by ignoring the strength of the peasants, General Chiang Kai-shek had lost a great opportunity.

The day after the awards, Pearl spoke to the Academy on the subject of the Chinese novel. Her address lasted an hour, followed by luncheons, teas and even a midwinter fiesta. Then the Swedish-American Society gave her a special dinner.

Worn out, she sailed home with her beloved Richard and her step-daughter. It had been, as Sinclair Lewis had prophesied, the greatest moment in her life as a writer.

Green Hills Farm

By this time the Walshes had transformed Green Hills Farm, located one mile west of Dublin, Pennsylvania, into a comfortable home for themselves and their ever growing family. The uncovered beams in the living room complemented the original floors found under layers of worn linoleum. Inside the panel of the upper section of a Dutch door, Richard was intrigued to find an inscription written in lead pencil: "On August 12, 1835, I married my true love, Magdalena." A grandfather clock that had come from Cliveden, the old Joseph Chew home in Germantown, Pennsylvania, could clearly be heard ticking away.

Richard once said that his wife would not be satisfied or feel truly at home until he made her a courtyard. This was accomplished in due time between the farmhouse and the original house behind it.

In the main library were shelves of children's books for the little ones. In the center was the original *Good Earth* desk on which Pearl had written her first successful novel. There was a Chinese chair by the table, together with two smaller folding Chinese tables.

Although Lossing Buck was given the contents of their Chinese home at the time of the divorce, the desk and some favorite rugs seem to have been returned to her—and possibly the chair.*

The rugs, made in Peking, arrived safely in New York City from China, though five rolls of them were somehow lost. Pearl complained to the American Express Company that it was incredible they could come that far safely from the Orient and then be misplaced in America. She gave them three months in which to find the rugs—and they did.

In addition to the main library, the Walshes had a private library which contained collector sets of Rudyard Kipling, Samuel Johnson, Walt Whitman, Henry Ibsen and Charles Lamb, together with books written by Pearl's favorite, Charles Dickens. A few volumes of the original set belonging to her missionary parents in China had miraculously survived years of revolution, looting and flooding. Until fifteen years of age, Pearl had read Dickens faithfully every year, particularly at Christmas time. In fact, it was Dickens's works that had most inspired her to become a writer. Often she told her adopted children how much she had cried when, at the age of five, she had first read *Oliver Twist* with her mother. In honor of Charles Dickens she had hung on the wall a poster from England's Rockingham Castle, where he was said to have written *Bleak House*. She had been visiting there when the owners,

* Although it is said not to be the one in which she sat to write *The Good Earth*, the author once had in his possession a 1930 snapshot of her sitting in what looks to be the same chair.

Sir Michael and Lady Faith Clume-Seymour, had given the poster to her.

Beyond the private library was Pearl's office and study, with a view from the window of ducks on the big pond at the bottom of the hill. The office opened into two greenhouses, one to supply cut flowers to brighten the cold winter days, the other, the Camellia House, in which to remember her favorite flowers back in China. A small fountain kept the air suitably moist. The Camellia House was one of Pearl's greatest pleasures.

The Walshes turned one upstairs hallway into a "Treasure Room," where they displayed Pearl's Nobel Prize medal and the large portfolio from the King of Sweden. Through the years they added many of the gifts and honors bestowed upon her. They devoted one whole closet to her doctoral robes, the thirteen hoods she had received for her honorary doctorates, and some of the beautiful Chinese brocaded jackets that she slipped into when she wanted to relax.

The children had free run of the house with the exception of their mother's writing room office. They learned early not to disturb her when the door was closed, for they knew she was working.

There were always secretaries to answer the enormous amount of fan mail, to say nothing of the countless requests Pearl received to speak. Miss Bucher, the official secretary, who had come from Nanking with Pearl and Janice in 1932, was eventually replaced by Richard's daughter, Natalie, who had married Bob Coltman. Natalie and Bob lived in a house nearby.

One project that Pearl and Richard especially enjoyed was editing Lin Yutang's new book *Moment in Peking*, which they later had the pleasure of seeing accepted by the Book-of-the-Month Club. Lin, with five family members, had arrived in America in September 1936, but immediately encountered prejudice. He attempted to lease a house belonging to the wife of a professor at Princeton University. Upon finding they were Chinese, the woman quickly broke their lease, which infuriated Pearl so much that she wrote a five-page letter, berating the woman for racial prejudice. Finally Lin's family settled in New York City.

Pearl had suggested she and Lin might work together on her play, *Flight into China,* which relates how the Chinese had welcomed Russian Jews during the Bolshevik Revolution, even intermarrying with them. However, the collaboration did not work out. Pearl decided that she was better at writing alone, and Lin seems to have agreed, so their friendship continued unchanged. He then completed his book, *The Importance of Living,* his second to be published in the United States. This, too, was chosen by the Book-of-the-Month Club.

War clouds were gathering around the world. In China, Chiang Kai-shek was beset not only by the Japanese invasion of his country but by the Communist threat from within the ranks of his own people. In Europe, the conflict between Britain and Germany was about to explode. While staying with Richard and the children in a house at Martha's Vineyard, Pearl learned of the war declared by Britain and her allies on Nazi Germany. Richard rushed over the dunes to break the disturbing news to his wife. Pearl recalled the moment vividly: "Our two babies, hand in hand, were running up and

Pearl Buck Residence—Green Hills Farm from 1934 to 1972.

Pearl's office at Green Hills Farm where she did her writing.

The original *Good Earth* desk and chair in the main library at Green Hills Farm.

The dining room at the Farm. Note the clock formerly owned by Joseph Chew—and the lonely irony of the single dinner setting in a home once filled with many happy children.

The living room where the author often met with Pearl and Richard. In the background is the main library.

down the beach in the shallow water, while the two little boys dug for sand crabs. Upon this scene, in spite of all its grace and calm, the war broke that day, and we knew, my husband and I, that our life would never be the same again, for war would change our country and our people. It would change, indeed, the whole world."

On December 7, 1941, when the Japanese bombed Pearl Harbor and forced the United States into World War II, Pearl's first thought was of Chiang Kai-shek—at last he would be helped in his desperate fight. Remembering her first meeting at Cornell with Eleanor Roosevelt, Pearl wrote the first lady, believing Mrs. Roosevelt to be a great influence on the President's thinking. She advised that the Asiatic peoples unfortunately considered white people their enemy and that they were "racially embittered" because of this. She emphasized that the sooner America's harsh immigration laws that discriminated against the Chinese were repealed, the better.

Mrs. Roosevelt must have been impressed with the letter from Pearl S. Buck, for when it was suggested in 1943 that she make a trip herself to China, she turned to the novelist for advice. The Franklin Delano Roosevelt Library archives at Hyde Park, New York, contain a letter from Pearl Buck to Eleanor Roosevelt dated March 22, 1943, regarding Eleanor's proposed visit to China. In it, Pearl outlines Chinese politics, likes and dislikes: "The Chinese people are really more appreciative of the simple human behavior. They catch instantly the friendly smile, the attitude of humility, the simple and human approach which is so essentially yours. I do not hesitate a moment to say, 'They would love you, Mrs. Roosevelt.'"

She proved her immense knowledge of Hankow, Chungking and various parts of China normally unknown to most American government personnel. Speaking of the Chinese leader, she also said: "Chiang cannot last if he continues in this aristocratic fashion.…What I am telling you is simply a synthesis of what I hear from many kinds of Chinese, particularly young Chinese.… I wish if you went to China you could get to know the real people. They are so quiet, so calm, so brave!"

She referred to her previous letter to Mrs. Roosevelt: "I told you that the Chinese are so much like us, you may remember and you wondered about that. I said that we have built the Chinese in our press like opera buffs…entirely false. They are amazed when they see it. They are so plain, so hearty, so wholesome that they cannot imagine where we get such notions of them. It is as if they were to picture us back in the eighteenth century with false masks, fantasy laden…pitter-patter and all that honeysuckle rosy-hued stuff and nonsense." She advised Mrs. Roosevelt: "Drink only bottled water.… It is perfectly polite to not eat everything offered."

In the ensuing years Pearl continued to make known her attitudes on foreign policy through telegrams to Mrs. Roosevelt, interceding for a Puerto Rican politician* and pressing for the release of Jawaharlal Nehru, who was then a prisoner of the British Empire in India. She cemented their friendship by sending grapes and farm produce to the President, who she knew was a gentleman farmer from Hyde Park in Dutchess County, New York. He never failed to reciprocate with a kind letter.

---

* Roosevelt instructed his attorney general to intervene on behalf of the politician; apparently Pearl's pleading *was* heard at the highest levels.

122   After World War II, Pearl attempted to interest American women in the plight of Japanese women affected by the bombing of Hiroshima. However, though she wrote to Senator Margaret Smith of Maine, Margaret Mead, Helen Douglas, Dorothy Canfield Fisher, Dorothy Thompson, Fleur Cowles and Eleanor Roosevelt, she could stir up little or no real interest. Because her own abundance of energy allowed her to accomplish so much, attending to even the minorest details, she could not understand others' lack of zeal. She was fond of saying, "Good Lord, deliver us from tired liberals." She then bombarded Dwight Eisenhower, Harry Truman, Adlai Stevenson, Henry Ford, Jr., Nelson Rockefeller, Henry Luce and Marshall Field—with equally poor results. Eventually she abandoned the project.

         Between them, Mr. and Mrs. Richard Walsh led full lives, overflowing with a young family, his publishing duties and her writing. They worked closely together from their adjoining offices at the farm.

         A large Chrysler car, complete with portable desk, dictaphone and typewriter, doubled as an office during their weekly trip to New York City. For years all major meetings concerning East Asia (such as the India League of America and the East and West Association) were held on Tuesday evenings. Most of these meetings took the form of banquets held at the Waldorf Astoria Hotel for such notables as Nehru's sister and daughter, Madame Pandit and Indira Ghandi. Pearl and Richard used the travel time to carry on their many business and writing interests.

         Richard protected his now famous wife by presiding over many press conferences for her in America and all over the world.

She commented: "He knew the reporters and they knew him. He was completely at ease at the first press conference he conducted for me...in New York City.... His natural ease made him a natural chairman and he was chairman of an amazing variety of organizations. How often...I watched him listen to every dissident voice, every argument, then quietly and in a few words gather the consensus of opinion into a resolution. He had the rare gift of creating order out of disorder. But beyond that he had the gift of human understanding which enabled him to select the essential from the inessential and to locate areas of agreement among those who disagreed."

In addition to managing his famous wife's public relations, he wrote a book of clever children's rhymes, a humorous mystery, a fine nonfiction piece on Marco Polo and his critical study of Buffalo Bill. But he still found time to teach the children to play tennis, baseball and golf.

Pearl, too, was associated with countless organizations, diverse as the Quaker Hostel in Harlem and the Provisional Committee to a Democratic Peace. She was eagerly sought as a luncheon speaker. Richard sorted through all the invitations and noted: "For twelve years now I have tried to guard the position Pearl Buck holds, so that her public usefulness will not be impaired by letting her be picketed or pigeon-holed. Just now it seems very important that her attitude on India and China and on race relations, which is unchangeable, does not appear to be anti-British, and that she does not drive wedges between us and our allies."

Her admiring neighbors in Bucks County even suggested once that she run for Congress, and Clifton Fadiman went so far in the *New Yorker* as to suggest she would make a good Ambassador to China. Gently, Richard discouraged both suggestions, explaining that "Mrs. Walsh feels she could be much more useful doing her own work in her own way."

The Walshes prized every moment together. Regretting that during the day they had to attend to their separate professions, they looked forward to the evenings. Wherever one went, the other accompanied, compromising on their own interests in order to savor every precious moment together. In the twenty-five years of their marriage they never spent a night apart. But even in their togetherness, they retained their own vibrant personalities. Pearl chafed sometimes at his distancing himself from household matters, which she stayed involved in no matter how busy she might be.

Their personalities were strikingly different. Richard displayed a keen, intuitive mind, appreciating what he could not comprehend. Pearl, on the other hand, loved science and searched out the answer to all mysteries of life in both science and world religion. When Pearl tried to change his mind about something, Richard would draw out his rough-cut tobacco, crush it in the palm of his hand, fill his beloved briar pipe and "smile in amusement with no intention to change." On the other hand, she said, "He loved to tell me jokes and stories. Since I had spent all the years in China he had much to tell me and I had much to catch up on. We never did get to the end of the jokes or stories as his fund seemed endless."

On occasion, Richard would evidence a feeling of jealousy. The first time it happened, Pearl angrily picked up one of the dozen beautiful antique plates they had brought from Europe and smashed it, threatening a repeat performance any time he

became jealous again. She never had to break another one and   125
the set of plates remained at an odd eleven.

Together they settled into a "comfortable organized
way of life casually organized around [their] work and the children." Of this happy time Pearl recounted, "We lived deeply. Our
pleasures were in music, in people, in the children, books and the
world of mountain, woods and the sea."

East and West Association

A s the United States plunged into World War II, Pearl plunged even deeper into her writing. She published the novels *Dragon Seed, China Gold* and *China Flight* in 1942 and *The Promise* in 1943. She wanted to explore the intricacies of love and marriage in the United States and, fearing her readers would not accept this change of pace, embarked on this new subject using the pen name of John Sedges. She gave several reasons for choosing to write under an assumed name. For one thing, she wanted to change her image from that of a woman who wrote only of Asia. She was absorbed in the way of life in this country and wanted to write its human stories as she had written of the common people in China. She also loved the anonymity of a pseudonym. Another reason advanced for Pearl's use of a pen name was that she loved writing so much that she couldn't restrain her efforts to only one or two books a year. But most of all the threat of McCarthyism was causing her own books to be sold from under the counter. The first novel under the John Sedges pen name, *The Townsman*, appeared in 1945.

Although the story takes place in Kansas, the hero of *The Townsman* was born in England. Kansans who read the book remarked that the book could only have been written by a Kansan. In planning her story, she laid out the town in keeping with her early lessons in the Chinese ethic of orderliness. She also employed what was for her an unusual technique. She wrote a natural catastrophe into the tale, using a prairie fire for drama as she had used the plague of grasshoppers in *The Good Earth*.

In 1945 she had experimented with a new type of writing which she called a "talk book." In this method of telling a story she carried on a dialogue with a person she felt had something to say to the American people. The dialogue was then transcribed and edited into a book. Her first two books in this format dealt with two different subjects: Russia and the Mass Education Movement in China.

The first book, *Talk about Russia: with Masha Scott,* was serialized in *Asia* magazine with the title "Talks with Masha." The serial began with the June 1945 issue. In it she tells of her first meeting with Masha, the wife of John Scott the *Time/Life* correspondent.

"I began to ask myself, 'What sort of people are the Russians now [at the end World War II]?' I have never been interested in politics because I do not consider politics basic. Politics, like religion, depends entirely upon the people behind them. It is the people I want to know...I must find a Russian, a real one, not a surface-skinned one, but someone who had grown up in this new Russia.

"They are not easy to find in the United States. First of all, I
had to eliminate any Communist, because Communists, like all
other human beings with causes and religions, are Communists
first. I wanted to find someone who was a Russian first.

"Then I thought of Masha. A short while before this I had
gone to a young American's house to dinner. I had heard that
John's wife was a Russian girl....We did not see Masha until John
said dinner was ready. Then Masha was there waiting for us...a
plain, forthright looking girl, Russian enough to have stood for
the symbol of all we think of as Russian...."

She was impressed with Masha's directness and
straight gaze and knew that Masha would be ideal for the book
that she had in mind. In the candid conversations that followed,
Masha called herself a "Collective," indicating that there was a
vast difference between that and being a Communist. She said
that a Collective has no political theory and belongs to no party
but is one who embraces a certain way of life, a practical system
of economics and agriculture. Masha was only a child when the
Red Russians defeated the White Russians in World War I and
accepted the common opinion that the Reds were their friends
and the Whites were their enemies. The most memorable
improvement she felt from the Revolution was the peasant's
opportunity to learn to read. All peasants could actually possess
reading matter whether newspapers, magazines or books. It
brought a feeling of equality.

Masha said that in the collectives, cooperation replaced competition. More people had a say in what was raised and how and
where. Her family was able to save and build themselves a new

house. Masha had been able to go to college to study chemistry and had attended operas and plays. When she graduated she took a job in Magnitogorsk, a planned city of new and exciting growth, open and bright. There she met John Scott, whose father and mother were university professors in the United States. Masha assumed that John had come to Russia to find work since the United States was in the throes of the Great Depression, but he actually had come to Russia to learn about the country from the ground up.*

Masha painted a glowing picture of post World War I Russia as she told of her family, her career and her marriage to John. Her description of Russia in the thirties led Pearl to conclude that: "The strength of Russia does not lie in her political theory. It lies in the fierce simplicity of her local realism. The people were oppressed and the oppressors were removed. The people were hungry and means were found to feed them....We must fight Communism by something better than Communism, something swifter, a quicker benefit to the hungry peoples, a wiser means. If the American way of capitalism, if the British way of empire cannot accomplish this, and in less than a generation, then Russia wins."

Some labeled *Talk about Russia* as "subtle Communist propaganda." Other reviewers hailed it as "the only objective book" written about that country.

---

* The author struck up a friendship with John after meeting him through Pearl Buck. At the time, John was traveling for *Life, Time* and *Fortune* magazines. He wrote the author faithfully, sending copies of his detailed reports to the publisher of *Time* on such topics as the Alliance for Progress, the Soviet world, peace in Asia, the Middle East at War and Detente. As the number one commentator on Soviet affairs, John Scott spoke to public and executive forums in Illinois, Arizona and Texas which the author arranged.

Pearl, however, was concerned, not with politics and ideologies, but with the fact that three-fourths of mankind were ill-housed, ill-fed and in ill-health. To her it did not matter who owned or controlled the third world. She was concerned with those who were taking an active part in alleviating the miseries of the downtrodden.

She turned to James Yen, the man who taught more people to read and write than any person in history, for her next "talk book." She had come to admire the man who, of all the Chinese intellectuals she knew, was the only one who had dedicated his entire life to the peasants of his country. In the book *Tell the People: Talks with James Yen about the Mass Education Movement,* she pointed out: "To work for peace as though it were a thing in itself is the crowning folly of our age. Oppression, hunger, ill-health and ignorance seldom bring peace."

James Yen was born of a scholarly father in the late 1890s in Szechuan. He walked ninety miles to his first school. Later he would walk three hundred miles to his high school at Chengtu. Still later he won scholarships at Oberlin College in Ohio and Yale University. He was inspired by the Nathan Hale statue at Yale to volunteer for service in World War I because of Hale's statement, "I regret I have but one life to give for my country."

There had been 200,000 Chinese peasants transported to France during World War I to help with construction. Yen volunteered to teach them to read and write since their illiteracy prevented them from writing or receiving letters from home. He reduced the 50,000 Chinese characters required for literacy in that language to 1000 and challenged the workers to learn these 1000 characters in four months. Soon his thousand-character system expanded into the Mass Education Movement in China.

Yen wrote: "Those with learning keep it for themselves and improve their own situation. Seldom do they think of it as something to be shared with all. That is the basis of my Mass Education Movement. There is much voluntary effort by those who have been helped to go on and help others. We have called it 'each one teach one' so that it multiplies." He used his movement to improve the lot of the poor peasants. He found that when he talked about railroads, they objected to it. If he talked about public health, they did not understand it. But if he talked about reading books, they understood that. It was something that had been denied the farmers. He enlisted the local leaders and teachers in his plans, convincing them that if their village was to be rich and strong it should be educated. He experimented with self-supporting People's Schools in the villages, finding that once the illiterate are informed, they want more than literacy. Eventually his movement spread to the entire Pacific basin. Of note is the fact that through his Rural Reconstruction work the province that gave the most resistance to the Communists in China was Szechuan, where Yen did most of his work.

Pearl always wrote in longhand and often let Richard help with the revision. He never let her down, submerging his own ambitions in hers. For relaxation she worked in clay, making rather professional looking heads of the children. She played her favorite Beethoven and Chopin on the piano and later bought an organ for the same purpose. As a popular speaker she received hundreds of speaking requests, receiving up to $1200 a lecture and never less than $500. Her correspondence alone required an entire staff of secretaries. Even so, she still regretted what she termed "my wasted years" between 1925 and 1935, grumbling that she had "the feeling of having spent part of my life in jail." "Why didn't I get to work?" she angrily asked herself.

But there was no time to dwell on the past, and in 1942 she founded the East and West Association for one purpose only. As stated on its letterhead, the Association's existence was "Devoted to new and better understanding between peoples East and West through mutual knowledge." The Association's Board of Directors and Advisory Board, though sometimes filled with prominent names, was mostly taken up by persons seeking better relationships between Asia and the Americas.

Early members of the Board of Directors included Juan Trippe, Henry Luce, Admiral W. F. Hoelsing, Perry Burgess, Louis Bromfield, Margaret Mead, Miguel Covarrubias, Edwin Reischauer, Mildred McAfee Horton and Paul McNutt—an impressive list by any standard.

Before East and West had grown to the point where it was able to support a magazine of its own, a special section of *Asia* magazine was dedicated to its concerns. The results of several polls, such as "Books of Americans That Asians Ought to Read" and "Films on America Asians Ought to See," were printed in the first issues. On the subject of "What Americans Should Asians Know Since 1900?" they listed such names as Woodrow Wilson, Jane Addams, John Dewey, Mark Twain, Henry Ford, Louis Brandeis, Oliver Wendell Holmes, George Washington Carver, Booker T.

Washington, Thomas Alva Edison, Luther Burbank, Helen Keller, Theodore Roosevelt, Franklin D. Roosevelt and Will Rogers.

The East and West Association had fine offices next to those of the John Day Company. One member of the large staff, Mary Tsuta Ohata Lombard, became a great favorite of Pearl. Half-Japanese, she was a graduate of Columbia University. Tsuta, as she was known, became associated with East and West as a concert singer, but in addition she gave to Pearl true friendship, something that was sadly lacking in the famous author's life. Later, Tsuta married Richard's son by his first marriage, Dick Walsh, Jr., to whom Pearl had confided, "There may be some finer person in the world than Tsuta, but if so I have never met one."

The East and West Association initiated an interchange of lectures and authors whose travel costs and other expenses were often quietly paid by Pearl herself. Even though she had a full staff attending to the Association's affairs, with her usual enthusiasm and attention to detail she was aware of the most specific details.*

One of the finest services performed through the East and West Association was to break the prejudice which had ensured that only European and North Americans performed in most concert halls. By introducing Central American, Latin American

---

* At the time, the author was Pearl Buck's national Field Secretary. It was his job to visit schools, colleges, universities and any other groups that would be interested in using the association's speakers and performers from throughout the world. In response to the author's reports, she wrote: "I read all your communications as they come into the office so I am fairly well posted on what you are doing. You have covered a lot of ground in a few months…that's good because we really have a brilliant group coming to perform for us again."

and Asian performers to American audiences, the Association proved that people were ready for such presentations, and performers from other countries were soon able to make their own contracts for future tours. In addition, many of these performers were scheduled at county and state fairs so the common people in America were exposed to the cultures of other countries. In turn, the visiting performers were able to get a closer view of the American people. A point was made to have United Nations members present at these fairs on the day their fellow countrymen were performing.*

For several years the East and West Association participated with the India League of America, presenting and honoring great Indians visiting the United States, such as His Excellency Asaf Ali, India's first ambassador, on April 15, 1948.

"Peoples East and West," a course lasting fifteen weeks, was given in many of America's largest cities including New York. Local education boards offered special credit to their teachers who participated. The National Broadcasting Company made a great contribution by presenting thirteen lectures on the air with an estimated audience of fifteen million listeners.

Chinese and American actors, dancers and musicians performed in each others' countries. Pearl admonished the visiting Asians: "You have nothing to teach, nothing to preach. All you have to do is be the best citizen of your country that you can, to represent what you would like Americans to think about your country."

In November of 1943 there were even Junior East and West Clubs popping up in schools across America. These were orga-

---

* The idea to present foreign performers at state and county fairs was the author's. It pleased Pearl enormously.

136 nized by teachers who had something more than tunnel vision at the height of World War II and were devoted to the ideals for which global war was being fought.*

Pearl also recognized the ideals for which the war was being fought. Her espousal of these ideals caused a five-year rift in her relationship with her beloved younger sister, Grace Yaukey. Grace and her husband Jesse, unhappy in their evangelical missionary lives, had embraced the Quaker faith and in so doing had become pacifists. While Pearl was patriotically involved with the war, her sister was not. And because of the emotional stress Pearl had suffered at the hands of missionaries, organized religion would remain distasteful to her for the rest of her life. She did not deny God, as her atheist husband Richard did; it was only some of His so-called servants that displeased her so much.

Constant errors in Hollywood-produced films about Asia and Asia Minor were a real sore spot with Pearl. She often commented on them in her column in *Asia* magazine. In the November 1942 issue was an intriguing article entitled "Films of America Asians Ought to See." The same issue criticized the Agnes Moorehead movie, *Journey into Fear,* for its improper Turkish costumes.**

---

* It's the author's opinion that people always seem to think "it'll work with youth." Yet, it worked only where dedicated teachers made it work. The author had two experiences in western New York State at this time. He tried in vain to interest persons in India, China and Burma, recalling two families who would not concern themselves with time, interest or study of southeast Asia. Their answers were, "It's none of our business. Let the missionaries worry about it." Each of these families later lost sons in the very area in which the author had tried to interest them in.

** Pearl Buck and the author often discussed the vast geographical misrepresentations that appeared in Hollywood movies. In one discussion, the author noted that the exciting movement of teakwood from being cut in the forests, lugged to the river by elephants, then floated downstream to be split into logs took years. The film *Moon Over Burma* crammed it all within the cinematic speed of one short season.

During this same East and West period, *Dragon Seed*, her novel dealing with the sufferings of the Chinese near Nanking during the horrific Japanese invasions, was filmed with Katherine Hepburn, Turhan Bey and Aline MacMahon as its stars. The movie was quite successful. A million people went to see it during its initial run at Radio City Music Hall in New York.

Unfortunately, the East and West Association, in spite of all the good it had done in fostering friendship between the nations involved, became the victim of Senator Joseph McCarthy, who intimated that it had become tainted by Communist infiltration, particularly among the Chinese artists. He waged a personal vendetta against both East and West and Pearl S. Buck, and she finally disbanded it.

Heartsick, she confided, "In addition to the McCarthy business, the discontent with Americans about Asia makes me feel that Americans do not want to see or hear about people from Asia. This has made me begin to believe that we in America will have to reach our maturity by the hard road of personal and material experience." These were prophetic words, for America's calamities in Korea and Vietnam were just around the corner.

In January 1949, the Central People's Government of the People's Republic of China took control of that vast war-ravaged land, forcing Chiang Kai-shek to flee to Taiwan. The new Communist China turned its back on the Western world. Through her writings, Pearl tried diligently to educate her fellow Americans on the value of keeping a dialogue with the Chinese people, advocating the value of trading with them. She cited America's closest wartime ally as doing just that when she wrote, "Britain follows this policy, but we Americans think that recognizing a government means approving it, which is straining at gnats and swallowing camels."

Back in 1943, while serving as vice chairman of the American Civil Liberties Union, in testimony before a California Senate Committee, Pearl condemned the confiscation of Japanese-American owned farmlands. This earned her a place on a list of "dangerous persons" who had aided the Communists, published by Republican Senator Jack Tenney, Chairman of the California State Senate Committee on Un-American Investigations. She was in good company with such prominent people as actor Danny Kaye, film director John Huston, Charlie Chaplin, Frederic March and his wife Florence Eldridge, Katherine Hepburn, Lena Horne and Langston Hughes.

Pearl S. Buck replied with characteristic dignity to her accuser: "I want to do more than merely deny that I am or have even been sympathetic to Communism. I am anti-Communist to the last drop of my blood. But this is far more than a personal matter. As a loyal and enthusiastic American, I say that the present activities of a few Americans are making our country a laughing stock for the whole world. Other peoples are amazed. They are asking if we are a nation of fools. True and honest Americans are filled with shame at what is going on. The lynching of Negroes in the South is no more evil, no more disgraceful to our country's good name than is this silly wholesale accusation now being made against random persons, high and low, ignorantly accusing them of Communism, fellow travellerism and whatnot."*

* Again she wrote to the author in response to a letter he had sent her, "I think you have expressed quite adequately my stand on Communism. The more I see of it the more it terrifies me and the more I have against it. Yet I realize that we have not always found the antidote to it. We cannot [find that antidote] unless we comprehend, better than we do, the practical conditions of the world."

It is interesting to note that on September 30, 1987, several years after the death of Pearl S. Buck, under the headline "FBI KEPT FILES ON U.S. LITERARY GREATS," Charles Trueheart, writing in the *Washington Post,* disclosed that "for more than fifty years, the FBI and other federal agencies gathered massive intelligence files on some of America's most distinguished writers, apparently because their work was considered subversive, suspicious or unconventional." Among them was Pearl S. Buck and, ironically, William Faulkner who had spoken so rudely of her when she had been awarded the Nobel Prize for Literature.

Of Pearl S. Buck, the FBI agency wrote, "Although it is not believed from information available that Mrs. Buck is a Communist, her active support of all programs advocating racial equality has led her to associate with many known Communists."

The FBI was grossly unjust in accusing her of being unpatriotic. Innuendos in the press, the frustration of endless denials, the financial losses she suffered, all had been precipitated by her vigorous stand on human rights! Raised in another land and returned to her own country, her enthusiastic patriotism was almost like that of a religious convert. In her 1937 essay entitled "On Discovering America," she enthused:

"In our diversity is our safety.... Ours is the only safe country in the world today, because we cannot be organized and regimented into any simple opposing forces. There are capitalists among the laborers and there are socialists among millionaires and their children....

"We give people a better chance than any other country because we believe in having a good chance ourselves. The result of all this is peace and opportunity. The opportunity for some to work, some to strike, some to succeed, some to fail and some to go on relief. In our diversity there is strength.

"Thus I feel we should forever welcome the restless, the bold, the brilliant and the good. We all have a right here, for America from the beginning has had all peoples, and her future depends on us all. We should teach our children that there is no final America yet, that they are making America too."

Her words have just as much meaning and just as vital a message today as they had half a century ago.

Welcome House

-ϩ CHAPTER 14

In 1946 Pearl Buck astonished the literary critics with the appearance of her new novel, *Pavilion of Women,* the subtle spiritual love story of Madame Wu, a high-born Chinese lady, and a renegade priest named Father Andre, defrocked by his church for his practical humanitarianism. When he is murdered while helping a wounded stranger, Madame Wu finds an affinity with the dead priest, knowing in her heart that one day they will meet again in heaven, for, as Pearl explained: "Love alone had awakened her sleeping soul and made it deathless.... She knew she was immortal." After *The Good Earth, Pavilion of Women* ranked second as a bestseller. It was also a Literary Guild Selection.*

* There were those close to Pearl who believed that the novel was somewhat autobiographical, reminiscent of a romance of the mind that she was thought to have had in China with the poet, Hsu Chih-mo, killed in an airplane crash some fifteen years before. One of the fictional Madame Wu's sons actually bore the name Chih-mo, and his death in the book is similar to that of Hsu Chih-mo himself. The newspapers had called him the Chinese Shelley.

But Pearl was not one to rest on her laurels. She brought out two more of her "talk books" in the next two years. The subject of one was Erna von Pustau, a German poet and writer who grew up in Hamburg, Germany. As a young woman she saw the rise of Nazism under Hitler. She revolted against the Nazi party, which led to her arrest and later to incarceration in a French concentration camp. The purpose of the book was to tell, as its title indicated, *How It Happens: Talk About the German People, 1914-1933*. Pearl hoped Americans would draw lessons from what happened to the German people and so be more alert and able to save the American way of life.

The other "talk book" was *American Argument: with Eslanda Goode Robeson,* who is well known, not only as the wife of Paul Robeson, the famous black singer and actor, but for her book *African Journey* and other writings. In the foreword to the book, Eslanda says: "As a Negro-American [sic], I have always bitterly resented the segregation and discrimination my country metes out to my people; but I have always resented this in a family sort of way. I have always known that I am as American as any other American, more American than some; not more so because I am American for three generations back, and because my grandfather as secretary of state and secretary of the treasury of South Carolina took part in the administration of some of my country, but more so because I have always believed in and practiced the laws, and the principles behind those laws, of my country. That certainly makes me a lot more American than some of my fellow citizens."

Pearl and Eslanda discuss their own country from differing and sometimes opposing, but always basic, points of view. Often they agreed, sometimes they disagreed sharply; it is a firm but friendly argument throughout.

During this period she also published two more novels
under the John Sedges pseudonym. *The Angry Wife* deals with
two brothers on opposite sides during the War between the States
and their love for two racially-mixed sisters. *The Long Love* is an
American love story in which Pearl explores the concerns of a
man who wants the most out of his job and the most out of his
marriage, and has to struggle hard not to sacrifice one to the
other. By this time she had already won a writing award for the
Sedges novel *The Townsman*.

Her novel *Peony* appeared under her own name and was based
on her ill-fated *Flight into China* research. As she explained: "At
various times in history colonies of Jews have gone to China and
lived there. The city of Kaifengfu, in the province of Honan, was
a center for them. In China they have never been persecuted, and
if they have suffered hardships, they were only the hardships of
life in the community where they were.

"In its basis, therefore, this novel may be said to be historically
true, although its important exceptions are the creatures of my
imagination. The story takes place at the period, about a hundred
years ago, when the Chinese had accepted Jews and when, indeed,
most Jews had come to think of themselves as Chinese. Today,
even the memory of their origin is gone. They are Chinese....

"All that is left of them is a few Jewish names, some relics, a
legend or two, the contour of a profile, the seemingly accidental
brilliance in an individual mind."*

* Coincidentally, when Pearl had first written about the Kaifengfu Jews in *Asia* magazine in 1943, the author was making an independent study of this same subject during
his graduate work on the history of Christian missions. The author had found a refer-
ence to them in some writings of Ricci, the great Jesuit missionary to China from
Rome, and wanted to know more about them. The result of his studies was his thesis
"The Jews of Kaifengfu;" the result of Pearl's studies was *Peony*.

Pearl's next major effort was *Kinfolk,* rumored to be based upon her old friend and former play collaborator, Lin Yutang. Sterling North quipped in the *New York Post,* "Pearl Buck has gently boiled in oil Dr. Liang (the hero)."

There was plenty of humor, favorably noted by reviewers, for Pearl's other books had been somewhat lacking in that capacity. Readers and critics alike adored the ancient Uncle Tao, who preserved his own tumor in a jar for everyone to see.*

In this story, which involves the four children of the Liang family, she uses her own experiences in reverse by having the Liang children, who had immigrated to America, decide to return to their homeland in China. Once again she gives a fascinating picture of the parallels of the two civilizations she loves and knows so well. It appears in the characters' attitudes toward marriage and family life, their fellow man, their jobs and their country. The likenesses and differences are the more poignant because they are incorporated in persons who have been shaped by the ways of the Occident and the Orient. As always in her books she weaves a tapestry from rich and poor, from intellectual and peasant, from agrarian and city sophisticate; and each person seems real. Humor, pathos and the larger emotions emerge.

Then came perhaps Pearl's most poignant piece of writing, an article for the *Ladies' Home Journal* about her retarded daughter Carol. So many parents of similar children were helped by this opening of her heart that the John Day Company later published it in book form under the original title, *The Child Who Never Grew.*

Pearl often took Carol to the farmhouse for visits although the

---

* Buck wrote this book during the author's association with her and it is one of the few personally autographed books of hers in his possession.

activity of such a large and varied household seemed to worry her daughter. In the end she bought a small house by the shore where they could spend time quietly together. Carol still had an affinity for her stepfather, and Richard reciprocated, loving her as tenderly as if she were his own. Pearl continued to give vast sums for research into Carol's malady. Eventually she was told that her daughter suffered from phenylketonuria, commonly known as PKU. Although the disease was reputedly inherited, Lossing Buck's two children by his second marriage were not afflicted.*

In Carol's case she could not absorb proteins necessary for normal development. By a strange coincidence, about the time that *The Child Who Never Grew* appeared, the wretched eczema from which Carol had suffered all her life nearly disappeared.

During Christmas of 1948, Pearl heard from an adoption agency seeking help in placing a fifteen-month-old boy of a missionary's daughter and an East Indian. Her parents had allowed her to bring the child home to America with the somewhat unchristian stipulation that she place it for adoption. Unfortunately, no one wanted a mixed-blood child, so a black orphanage was the only alternative.

When Pearl asked the ever-understanding Richard what to do, he replied, "It doesn't seem right to let him go to that orphanage. We

---

* Lossing Buck married a Chinese woman named Lomay Chang with whom he had two children. Lossing's second marriage was a happy one. He stayed in China with his new family until conditions there forced them to leave in 1944. He returned later to give his considerable expertise to China's post war restoration under the direction of the China-United States Agricultural Commission. With his family, he then went to Rome as head of the United States Food and Agriculture Organization. Later, in 1954, he oversaw the formation of the Council on Economic and Cultural Affairs, whose main interest was directed to the Far East and other parts of Asia. The council had been set up by John D. Rockefeller III.

must do whatever we think right." So a very frightened little David arrived at the farmhouse, so petrified that he couldn't even cry. Pearl sat up with him for most of the night, holding his little hand.

David was hardly settled when another baby arrived, fathered by a Chinese doctor and born to an American nurse. Realizing that she could not adopt all these babies herself, Pearl tried to find them good homes through reputable adoption agencies but was always met with rejection because "we cannot match parents." She soon concluded that the growing number of Amerasian children born as the result of World War II could not be placed by the existing agencies. She wrote to the officials of the Army, Navy and Air Force, even the Department of State: "It is particularly difficult for Americans to understand how a half-white or half-black child stands out among people of one color and one type of hair. They look oriental when brought to America, but they look American while in Asia. I am particularly sensitive to this as I grew up in Asia as a white child among Chinese people and though they were kindly and curious, their comments on my hair and eyes, let alone color of my skin, left me with a feeling of desolation and isolation."

The government officials all replied that it was not their problem! Pearl felt that it was indeed every American's problem. She was certain that the importance of American relations with oversees countries could not be overstated. From personal experience she knew that enough people dislike Americans without adding the additional problem of American fathers abandoning their half-caste children in these countries.

Finally, a furious Pearl S. Buck took drastic action. "I was indignant so I started my own agency," she said.

They called it "Welcome House," and as always, she tells her own story best: "Before we proceeded we talked with members of the county. Would they welcome these children? Would they stand behind them when they came of age? Would they help others not to show prejudice because of half-Asian blood? One Pennsylvania Dutch grocer said, 'We not only want them, we will be proud to have them.'

"With this assurance we went to our state capital and asked to be chartered as an adoption agency. They had never heard of Amerasian children. Was there a need? In no time at all they discovered by checking that although the numbers were not yet considerable, it did make these children the greatest problem adoption agencies had. We were given our charter and we set up for business.

"I must say that long ago Asia helped me to understand the value of these children. I had the conviction that they were worth every effort. My experience is that the mixed blood, hybrid, human being is usually better than either side. I had seen hundreds of such hybrid persons in Asia, as the white man usually scatters his seed wherever he goes. I had always been impressed by hybrid beauty and brains. Dr. George Snell, an American geneticist, had confirmed this opinion by declaring that all great civilizations have come from hybrid peoples. We Americans are a mixed people and much of our energy and brilliance comes from our mixtures. Beyond the human range witness the hybrid rose and the hybrid corn. It is wise, I believe, to see that hybrid human beings are also given every opportunity. Moreover, I have seen in Asia the evil effects of prejudice upon such persons and from both sides of their ancestry. I could not bear to see prejudice work its way here, too. It is dangerous in any country to subject its superior individuals to prejudice. Good brains under such circumstances can backfire into special mischief.

"It was not easy nevertheless to get our first child adopted. He was neither of the two I have mentioned, for other children began to come to us as our agency became known. We had nine children before one was adopted. But we did find parents for them—one pair of parents for all nine in fact. They were a warm-hearted Pennsylvania Dutch couple—the Yoders. With these foster parents our first nine have lived happily and with every opportunity a loving family can give.

"Then came our tenth child, a little half-Japanese boy, who won my heart with his smile when he first saw me. Someone must surely want this child, I thought. I took him home from a western city where I had to fetch him. For two months I did my best to find adoptive parents for him, but in vain. One night I was speaking before a vast audience of well dressed, intelligent people. I decided suddenly to appeal to them on behalf of my little boy. Before I began my formal address, I told his story simply and put the question to them, 'Isn't there somewhere in this audience a young couple who wants this baby?'

"I had a letter the next day from a young minister and his wife. They wanted the baby. We soon were friends. I warned the pastor the time might come when a half-Japanese son would be a hazard to him. Some Christian church where he hoped to go might decide against him because of the child.

"'I have faced that,' he said firmly.

"They took the baby after all the formalities had been

observed and the legalities carried out. It was several years later when the young minister applied for a church in another state. He wrote that he had a half-Japanese adopted son. The reply came that the church officials had sifted down all applications to two, and these two remaining were so nearly equal that the vestrymen would not have known how to choose except that one said he had a half-Japanese adopted son. This was the deciding factor—they wanted such a pastor. I tell this because I want everyone who reads this to know we also have such people in our country."

In the ten years that followed more than one hundred babies were placed by Welcome House in homes throughout the United States. Not a single child was deemed to be too weak in mind or in body with the exception of one injured at birth. They were all fine children, most of them far above average, several with IQs in the genius range.

Sumi Mishima Gerhart was one of those fortunate Amerasian children to be chosen early to live at Welcome House. She recalls that Pearl was familiarly known as "Gran" and Richard was always "Grandaddy." The children were taken to Green Hills Farm for swimming, tennis and ice skating. They loved to play in the great barn, and eagerly anticipated the family gatherings at Halloween and Christmas.

Pearl was greatly helped in the creation of Welcome House by her neighbors Margaret Fischer and her Philadelphia industrialist husband, Kermit; this kind couple had two adopted children of their own. The Board of Directors of Welcome House included David and Lois Burpee of the Burpee Seed family, Broadway producer Oscar Hammerstein II and his wife Dorothy (Pearl had met him at the Authors' League of America) and Dr. and Mrs. Frederick Stamm.

Pearl asked Mr. Hammerstein to be the board's first president and Mrs. Burpee, who donated an office at the Ford Hook Farm for the venture, to act as treasurer. Pearl herself served as Chairman of the Board and personally interviewed existing adoption agencies to determine what was needed.

The board members were versatile in the way they raised money to support their new venture. Mrs. Hammerstein gave a gala fashion show in her garden where Kitty Carlisle was the most popular of models. Oscar Hammerstein, while president of Welcome House, received a "welcome" sixtieth birthday gift from his colleague, composer Richard Rodgers, who paid off the mortgage on the new Welcome House property.

Lloyd and Viola Yoder, the warm-hearted Pennsylvania Dutch couple who were the foster parents of the first nine children, took on the added responsibility of managing Welcome House. Once again, Pearl not only supported Welcome House with funds but attended its annual meeting with the adoptive parents each summer.

The East and West Association and Welcome House were projects of international scope. But Pearl was equally interested in the needs and concerns of her own countrymen.

When Elisabeth Waechter, a dedicated special education teacher, founded a school for retarded children in Eugene, Oregon, she wrote to ask permission to name her new school The Pearl Buck Center.

In her foreword to *A Community Success Story* in which she later wrote about this school, Pearl says: "The Pearl Buck

School—I tried the name upon myself. Not a very euphonious name for a school! I have never liked my own name. Why perpetrate it upon others? Nevertheless it is the only name I have. And the retarded children? They have a special place in my heart and my life. Yes, the heart said. Therefore yes it was. I wrote in my reply that I would be honored to have my name so used." This was the only time she ever agreed to have her name used on something other than her own enterprises.

No need was too small to merit her attention. In 1948, during the worst flood of the century in the Pacific Northwest, Vanport Community College (the forerunner of Portland State University) in Portland, Oregon, had its library flooded out. This occurred while Dr. Jean Black, its head librarian, was attending the annual American Library Association meeting in Atlantic City, where Pearl was a featured speaker. Having to leave the meeting early to return to Portland because of the flood, Dr. Black mentioned to Pearl that the entire library had been destroyed. Pearl offered to send autographed copies of every one of her books that had been published to date to initiate the task of starting a new library from scratch. True to her word the entire collection arrived at that little library within a short time.

Pearl Buck's actions are the best testimony of her devotion to her fellow human beings.

Vermont

⤳ CHAPTER 15

P earl's romance with the state of Vermont began in 1949, when she and Richard were invited to visit the home of John Scott's father, Scott Nearing. Nearing had written a book on harvesting maple sugar for the John Day Company.

The green hills of Vermont reminded Pearl of China, and the fresh air did wonders for her ragweed allergy. She decided that a summer home would be good for their growing sons, so she bought land on which they could build a concrete and stone house. An area native, Richard Gregg, helped them. It took three years for the stone house to be built. During that time, Pearl and Richard's adopted children thoroughly enjoyed their rustic adventure, with wildcats, bears and an occasional lynx for neighbors. When Janice visited the family, she found her famous mother pumping water and doing the cooking just as the Pilgrim mothers did; in a pot hanging from a huge crane in the open fireplace.

Later, Pearl also purchased an old house into which she put running water. Then she obtained more land with a fine view of Stratton Mountain, where she decided to build what she called her "dream house." The contractor thought she was quite mad when she presented him with the plans; one side was to be built right into the mountain with plenty of windows on the remaining three. However, as the contractor soon learned, one did not argue with Mrs. Walsh, and "Forest Haunt" was built to her specifications.

Shortly before Forest Haunt was finished, the Walshes called on a new neighbor, Jackie Breen and her husband George. The Breens had just moved to Vermont from Connecticut and were totally unprepared for a visit.

Jackie was in the middle of housework when the Walshes' enormous chauffeur-driven black limousine pulled up at her door. She was quite nervous when she asked them in, but Pearl and Richard soon put her at ease. Jackie vividly remembers the visit.

"She and Mr. Walsh called on us just a few weeks after we moved into our maple farm about one mile from Forest Haunt. Since we were not fully unpacked, I offered them tea and still remember my embarrassment having to serve it in plastic cups."

To Jackie, Richard seemed almost youthful with his crew cut hair. Pearl, she noted, was pleasantly plump. Pearl had apparently been appraising the Breens as well, for she immediately asked if they would like to work for her.

Happily, the answer was yes. Pearl hired Jackie as her secretary and George as her Vermont business manager. In those days, Pearl answered every scrap of mail she received and there was plenty of work for both to do.

Among her other duties, the new secretary was given complete instructions for the decorations that would finish Forest Haunt. These she carried out to the letter, much to Pearl's satisfaction.

Working for Pearl opened new vistas for Jackie Breen, who recalls, "She [Pearl] was an accomplished pianist and when I walked toward her home through the sugarbush, I could hear her practicing from afar. Had she not chosen to be a writer, I always felt she could have become a concert pianist.

"She was working diligently on her play about the scientific possibility of transmitting humans through space such as one sees on "Star Trek."* One evening, I went to the drive-in theater and saw the picture *The Fly,* which was about the very same idea. She seemed disbelieving, but later had to change the play. We travelled to New Haven for the opening, but it bombed. She seemed very low that evening."

One thing Pearl had never forgotten or forgiven was the way she had been demeaned by Faulkner and some of the other Nobel Prize winners. This slight she mentioned more than once to Jackie Breen, who said, "They treated her with resentment that she, a mere woman, should be among them."

Although H. L. Mencken had dubbed Pearl S. Buck as "that idiot," millions of women, not only in America but around the world, read and doted on her every word. In reviewing *The Hidden Flower,* Pearl's love story about an American G.I. and a Japanese girl, fellow writer Elizabeth Janeway was vigorous in her commendation: "She [Pearl S. Buck] is not an idiot. If our mores

---

* Apparently, some scientist friends had shared with Pearl the possibilities of this, and as she was always excited about new and different concepts, she decided a play would be the medium to explore such a possibility.

are changing in the direction of tolerance, if our knowledge of the world is broadening, it is she who is accepting the change. It is vital to communicate with this woman, for if literature has first of all the duty of reflecting life truly (I don't mean photographically), it has the second duty of presenting the reflection to as large an audience as possible. For twenty years Miss Buck has done this. It is an excellent thing that she continues to do it so well."

In 1951 Pearl, then fifty-nine, and Richard, sixty-seven, adopted another child, Henriette, whose circumstances did not qualify under their charter for admission to Welcome House. Five years old and stubborn, she was the child of a black American army officer and a German mother. Much discriminated against in her mother's native village, she could not speak any English upon her arrival at Green Hills Farm. As she grew, her nature was so like Pearl's that her new mother would say with much pride, "Henriette is more like me than any of the others."

Even with the move to Vermont and the care of the adopted children, Pearl continued turning out two novels a year. *Voices in the House,* the last of five books to use the John Sedges pseudonym, was a novel set in Vermont. It was a mystery of a sort, interweaving the influence of the servants' lives upon the owner of the house. In it she explores the differences between a man and a woman: "Her passion was a secret silver spring permeating all her being, connecting nerves, feelings—while his was a river separate and strong. The river flowed independent of all else. The spring in her could be stopped by dictate, moods and thoughts she concealed."

Serious conversation seemed impossible for the family in this story. They would sacrifice their souls for wisecracks, a form of speech Pearl Buck personally thought was not only destructive to the family but to civilized persons in general. That she was able to create characters who could do it successfully was a pointed indicator of her vast talent for getting inside the hearts and heads of other people.

After Pearl completed her autobiographical *My Several Worlds,* the Walsh family drove west for a long-planned trip. They took along a portable stove and a small refrigerator. Pearl was the cook, and, in the evening, along with her daughter Jean, she became the dishwasher. The children were all delegated to write reports on what they had seen for the family newsletter. With their faithful chauffeur Ottinger as the driver, the Walsh family finally arrived in Sheridan, Wyoming.

In Sheridan, Richard suffered what was thought to be a slight heat stroke, so it was decided that the children should be taken to see Yellowstone Park while he and Pearl rested. But the rest did little to ease the effects of the stroke.

Home again, with his speech still slurred and his face drawn, Richard consulted his own doctor. He seemed back to normal in a couple of weeks, but not for long. The sight in one eye started to go, and then, as Pearl sadly wrote, "Month after month, slowly his health deteriorated, but he never complained, patiently sorry to give so much trouble."

In the summer of 1954, when they went to see their new house, Jackie Breen was shocked at Richard's gaunt appearance, remembering the virile man with the crew cut she had met on his first visit to her home. He had since become such an invalid that Pearl now had to help him through the front doorway. She struggled to recapture the vitality of their marriage, changing her customary "Pearl S. Buck" signature to "Mrs. Richard Walsh" on all her personal correspondence.

It was obvious that Richard had a terminal illness. The doctor warned his wife that death might be imminent or it might be years away. In the evenings she read their favorite books to him, then played the piano. When his eyesight worsened, he tried to learn to read in Braille, but to no avail. Pearl describes the slow ebbing of his gentleness. "He continued as he had always been, lovable, patient, unwilling to cause trouble until the inevitable time when the disease ran its course, and there could be no more communication as the brain was dead to all appearances. Thus language was lost, eyesight failed and the brain seemed to go to sleep.

"Slowly the end came. When he could no longer read we went for the Library of Books for the Blind. They were most helpful, but when the mind could no longer absorb, even this avenue was cut off. So, too, with the music."

As she faced the new, inevitable solitude, Pearl recalled how much they had enjoyed attending the theater. Now she would have to go alone. She recollected his love for Gilbert and Sullivan, which she did not particularly appreciate but adapted to, just as he adapted to some of her classical music choices. She realized then that just as one acquired musical ability by steady practice, now she would have to practice the art of solitude. The ultimate tragedy for Pearl encompassed the times when a book was finished and he could no longer remember to say, as he had so often on similar occasions, "This is a big day."

Yet somehow she continued with her writing and helping unfortunate children. She was working on a novel using the research for her never-produced play. The novel, about China's last Empress, was to be called *Imperial Woman.* There was even talk of it being made into a motion picture, a project which never came to fruition.

Green Hills Farm never lacked the sound of children's voices. Miki Sawada, a Japanese woman who had herself rescued many deserted children, begged "Miss Pearlbuck," to find room for yet another child. In due time this time the little girl, half black and half Japanese, arrived. She was adopted and named Chieko Walsh. Soon she was followed by two others, Johanna and Teresa.

When well-meaning friends asked why in middle age she felt that she had to take on so much extra responsibility, Pearl was apt to revert to one of her favorite Chinese proverbs, "Give a man a fish, and you feed him for a day. Teach a man to fish, and you feed him for a lifetime."

In the first stages of his illness, Richard had made Pearl promise to lead as normal a life as she could under the circumstances. Above all, she was to continue writing, which he considered her very lifeblood.

David Lloyd, her friend and trusted agent, died in 1956 and was succeeded by Dorothy Olding. The *Ladies Home Journal* saw fit to reject Miss Olding's first submission for her prestigious client, titled "The Crucifixion." It seemed to upset the embarrassed new agent more than it did the author.

160 About this same time Pearl became president of the Authors Guild, a position which she held most successfully. Pearl was extremely popular with other Guild officers and members and her name alone was an asset to the organization.

Among Pearl's friends was Isabel Lydia Whitney, America's first woman fresco painter and a watercolorist of repute. (Miss Whitney was the cousin of John Hay Whitney, American ambassador to Britian.) Although Miss Whitney enjoyed her visits, Pearl never gave her much advance notice—usually calling the same morning and asking that Isabel find her chauffeur a parking space for her car. As parking was always a problem on New York City's popular West Tenth Street, Miss Whitney and her elderly staff, (including an Italian major domo) were hard pressed to know what to do. In desperation, Miss Whitney once telephoned the local precinct to announce, "This is Miss Whitney. Pearl S. Buck is coming to tea and needs a parking place." In no time two policemen turned up to erect two signs in front of the mansion. They each read: "NO PARKING TODAY, FUNERAL."

Richard Walsh's Death

The movies and television were rapidly becoming the first choice of entertainment for America, and Pearl's books were frequently considered for adaption to film. *Letter from Peking,* the love story of an American woman and a Chinese, was well received by the critics then optioned for a movie. The theme was announced by Pearl as taken from her own life experiences. The American woman and her Chinese husband are separated by the Communists and she returns to live in Vermont with their son. In his mother's homeland, the son encounters racial animosity. The father meanwhile has been forced to take a Chinese wife and later is shot while trying to join his family in America. Written to touch the emotions, the story succeeds admirably but was never made into a movie.

Part of *My Several Worlds* had been sold for television. CBS would produce the movie with Tad Danielewski, who had trained for the theater in Berlin, as director. Pearl would narrate.

Filming went smoothly until the last day, when the program manager decided that the result was not commercially suitable. Changes were ordered that upset Danielewski very much. Pearl said, "He was crushed."

Shortly after, Danielewski left CBS for NBC, and from his new office contacted Pearl with a program idea. Danielewski's sensitive approach to her material was not lost upon its author. To Pearl's delight, the resulting television adaptation of *The Big Wave* received critical acclaim. Then, for television's "Robert Montgomery Show," Pearl wrote "The Enemy," based on a short story she had written for *Harpers* in 1942. Again Danielewski directed. The reviews were excellent and she and Danielewski became close friends.

Their next business collaboration was for a Broadway play. She had told him about the play she had written concerning an atomic scientist, and Danielewski encouraged Pearl to improve upon its theme. Richard, housebound, encouraged their efforts so that when research took her across the United States, she felt confident in leaving others to care for her sick husband and their farm home. After weeks of hard work, *A Desert Incident* was finished, but they were unable to find a producer.

Meanwhile, the John Day Company badly needed another Pearl S. Buck book, so she obliged them with *Command the Morning*. The plot of this story was built around atomic energy and the death of a scientist by radiation. Her work in researching the book was praised by atomic scientists as being exceptionally accurate.

Pearl's energy in middle age was amazing. However, the unproduced play was still her dearest obsession, so she spent hours at a time working with her director, Danielewski, in revision and cutting. When they still were unable to place *A Desert Incident,* they formed their own production company, Stratton Productions— so named for her favorite Vermont mountain.

The play finally opened in New Haven, Connecticut and ran for twenty-one performances. But at the end it still badly needed work. Try as they might, Pearl and Danielewski were unable to give the play that magical essence that is required of a successful stage production.

A Desert Incident finally made its ill-fated Broadway debut March 24, 1959. The critics were unusually brutal. The *New York Daily Mirror* dubbed it the "worst play of the season" and "absolutely ridiculous," while Richard Watts condemned it as "probably the worst." Brooks Atkinson of the *New York Times* called Pearl's intentions good, but even his kind words could not save it.

Pearl was outraged, but she simply would not accept defeat, and so one theatrical disaster followed another. The next catastrophe was the resurrection of her old script, *My Indian Family.* This time she decided to create a musical. The result was *Christine,* starring the popular Hollywood actress, Maureen O'Hara. It ran on Broadway during May of 1960 but bleakly expired after only twelve performances.

The next project was the making of a film based on the successful NBC production of *The Big Wave.* Joining forces with the Japanese Toho film production company, Stratton Productions' Tad Danielewski and a representative from the Toho company would be co-directors. Pearl went to Japan for the filming, but her expertise soon required her to remove the Japanese director. Danielewski, she announced, would direct alone.

In the midst of her work, a telephone call from one of her daughters conveyed the news that Richard was dead.

Pearl was unable to get a plane back to America for some hours, so, in the interval, she visited Miki Sawada's orphanage. Even with her mind on Richard and their happy years together, his widow had a kind word for each of the 148 children she met that day.

Reassurances from friends and from Richard's own doctor, who had said that Richard wouldn't know if she were home or not, had persuaded Pearl to carry on with her busy life and go to Japan. But she felt somewhat guilty at not having been at his side when he died.

Once on the plane home, she felt the need to talk to somebody and discovered that the stranger beside her also had a retarded daughter. He was equally surprised when Pearl said, "Much of my life has been spent working with retarded children and their parents. This has been my destiny because, you see, my only earth child is retarded."

The words of another passenger were comforting. This man was a scientist on his way to an assignment in Washington, D.C. Pearl recalled, "As I listened to the man I was reminded that it was as if Richard himself were reminding me that life could go on with the varied interests we had shared. Science was but one of those. He seemed closer than ever before." She thought of her fellow author Rumer Godden's book *The River,* which includes the quotation, "The beginning is the end and the end is the beginning."

The funeral service was held at Green Hills Farm. Pearl stood beside her sister Grace as the minister, Dr. Frederick Stamm, led the mourners. Although Richard professed to be an atheist, he had always liked Dr. Stamm. Pearl was silent as the funeral procession made its four-hour journey to the Walsh family burial plot in New Rochelle, New York.

Back again at the farm, Pearl took three of her adopted daughters—Henriette, Johanna and Chieko—for a holiday in Vermont, where an avalanche of sympathy letters and telegrams followed. She did not stay long, for her ever active mind was back in Japan with *The Big Wave*. Finally she returned to the set, as she said, "to observe."

When the filming was completed, Pearl and her friend Miki Sawada visited Korea* at the invitation of a large magazine. She was appalled at the number of unwanted children of Korean mothers that American G.I.s had fathered.

Unfortunately for Stratton Productions, *The Big Wave* had the somewhat dubious distinction of only being screened once, near Pearl's home in Bucks County. Allied Artists and other distributors wanted no part of it. One wonders why Pearl did not devote her great energies, which she jokingly would say were derived from drinking ginseng tea, only to her books instead of the theater.

Pearl's next project was a book dedicated to Richard's memory. Entitled *A Bridge for Passing*, it was well received by critics and public alike and helped many people recover from the loss of a loved one. Describing her husband's last illness, she wrote: "Resolutely cheerful and happy, he never suspected the ultimate tragedy that befell him. He knew many very rich people and gave endlessly to the poor. If I said anything, he would say, 'They mean no harm.' The very rich did not come to his aid the only

* The Koreans almost literally killed her with their kindness, serving kimchi that made her violently sick.

two times he needed them in our twenty-five years together. Instead he resolutely faced the problem grimly and independently. The Chinese have a saying that of the thirty-six ways to escape problems, running away is the easiest. He never ran away."

She admitted in *A Bridge for Passing* that some of her biggest arguments with Richard concerned life after death. She once wrote: "For me death is merely the entrance into further existence. I do not know what that existence will be, but then I did not know what existence in this stage would be when I was born into it. I did not ask to be but I have been and am. My reason tells me I shall continue to be. I am on my way somewhere, just as I was on the day of my birth.

"There will be those who question my certainty of a continuing existence. My belief is based upon sound scientific reasons and long acquaintance with some of the greatest scientists and philosophers of our time. Religious faith and scientific hypotheses are much nearer to the same conclusions than is commonly realized."

After Richard died, the apartment they had shared was scheduled for demolition, so one of her daughters helped her find another. They narrowed the prospects down to three, and in the darkness of night she randomly picked one. Speaking of it in her conclusion to *A Bridge for Passing,* she says with a note of hope:"I am beginning to believe there is no such thing as pure chance in this world. When I was a child and often reluctant to do my duty, my father used to say to me firmly but gently, 'If you will not do it because it is right, then do it for the greater Glory of God.'"

The truth of his words was brought home when she opened the door of her new apartment. Because through its windows, she was confronted by the words carved in huge stone letters upon the building opposite, AD MAIOREM DEI GLORIAM.

Pearl would explain: "They face me now as I write. 'To the greater glory of God!' What does it mean, this voice from the grave, my father's grave? He lies buried on a mountaintop in the very heart of a China lost to me. I am here and alone and thousands of miles away. Are we in communication, he [Richard] and I, through my father? It is not possible."

One wonders.

Pearl S. Buck Foundation

⮷ CHAPTER 17

Pearl looked around for something to fill the void created by her loss. She determined to make the best of what years remained to her, and as a symbolic reentry into her new life, she began to close her letters once more with the famous "Pearl S. Buck" signature. When the opportunity came for Stratton Productions to make a film in India, Pearl was intrigued with the idea. The film was to be called *The Guide*.

Pearl arrived in India February 16, 1963, with Danielewski and his young Midwestern assistant, John Anderson. They were warmly greeted by Nehru, who took the opportunity to praise the memory of Richard Walsh as being "one of God's true gentlemen." Pearl noted, "It seemed ironic that Richard had been an atheist."

Pearl liked to brag that it was Richard who had first brought the great books by India's leader, Jawaharlal Nehru, to the American public for her late publisher husband "had the gift of universal comprehension, an eclectic mind, a synthesizing judgment, enlivened by faith in talent wherever he found it."

During her stay in India, Pearl arranged to interview the Dalai Lama of Tibet for two articles commissioned by the *Ladies Home Journal.* She found the religious leader "very refreshing."

Pearl carefully made notes for the new Indian novel she was planning, to be entitled *Mandala.* There were production problems with *The Guide* as there had been during the filming of *The Big Wave* in Japan. At times the leading man, Dev Anand, on whom she was purportedly basing the hero of *Mandala,* was most unhappy, as was his company, which had poured millions into the project.

John Anderson, with his good common sense, proved to be a strong mediator during all the squabbling. He was kindness itself to Pearl, who left alone for even a short time became noticeably distressed. She later described what she feared once the film would be completed: "I wondered what would take the place of those months of working and living in so vivid a country." As it turned out, they left India before the film was finished.

Pearl continued to put money into Stratton Productions for some time to come, doubling Ted Danielewski's salary when he wed aspiring actress Priscilla Decator in Philadelphia. John Anderson escorted Pearl to the ceremony, which was held in a beautiful garden. Of her friendship with the bridegroom, Pearl somewhat testily noted, "We made two beautiful motion pictures together, having unforgettable experiences that some stupid people are not even capable of understanding."

Now home, she quickly finished writing *Mandala.* From time to time Pearl had hinted that she was interested in reincarnation, extra-sensory perception (ESP) and the age-old preoccupation with the self, topics now referred to as "New Age." *Mandala* was a chance to investigate these phenomena. The word "mandala" means "a schematized representation of the cosmos, chiefly characterized by a concentric organization of geometric shapes, each of which contains a deity or an attribute of deity. It is a symbol representing the effort to reunify the self."

In the story, Pearl explores the mysticism that pervades everyday life in India. Any sojourner there soon learns how pervasive this mysticism is, a mysticism which appealed to Pearl Buck's intuitive powers. The story is centered upon a modern princely family of the New India. ESP, reincarnation and spirits are very real concerns of the Maharana Prince Jagat. For the first forty years of his life the prince had been content to spend his passion on tiger hunts. As the novel opens, political events have stripped him of his wealth and titles but not of his responsibility to the local villagers. Now he has determined to turn his opulent but ghost-ridden lake palace into a luxury hotel for tourists. When news reaches him that his only son has been killed by the Chinese in a border clash, his life changes even more. Convinced that Jai's spirit lives, he sets off to find his son's remains. This leads him into a new life with many strangers he otherwise would not have met.

Pearl also planned new outlets for her energies. Work alone was not enough to fill the void left by the death of Richard. She would take French lessons and ballroom dancing. (Ironically, towards the end of her life Pearl's mother Carie had complained that she had become a missionary instead of first learning to dance properly.)

At this time in her life, Pearl was also blessed with the devotion of a man *Time* magazine had affectionately called "The People's Philosopher." His name was William Ernest Hocking—"My Ernest...my Best Beloved" as she would address him in the many letters they would exchange. The government of West Germany had conferred upon him the Order of Merit and among his many talents was the gift for writing.

He had sent Pearl a book, *Thoughts on Death and Life*, written in memory of his late wife. After receiving it, Pearl visited him in his New Hampshire mountain-top home. Hocking was then over eighty but, as she noted, looked at least twenty years younger and had the bluest eyes she had ever seen. From the early nineteen sixties until his death on January 27, 1966, they became very dear to one another.

Pearl told her sister Grace that Ernest Hocking had proposed marriage to her but that she could not face the risk of seeing him visibly deteriorate as Richard had done. To her "Best Beloved Ernest" she wrote that she wished they had met when they were both young, but confessed that at that time she might not have been ready for his brilliant mind. She blamed this opinion on her own personality, "for it is not easy to cope with a temperament, an imagination, even a talent, if you will, such as God and ancestry have bestowed upon me. It has been like trying to drive to capacity, and yet in orderly fashion, a team of too many horses!" It was to Ernest Hocking's ample library that she retired to research more material as the background to *Mandala*.

It seemed that there was no Far Eastern country that Pearl would not tackle in her writings. She focused upon Korea in her novel *The Living Reed*, so it seemed appropriate during a White

House dinner given for Nobel Prize winners that President John F. Kennedy would question her about that country. She promised to send him a copy of her book, which she thought might answer his questions.

"Alas," she later recalled, "when the first copy came off the press in 1963 and I sent it to him, he had gone to Texas."

She later wrote a sympathetic book, *The Kennedy Women* (which carried an advance of $75,000), comparing them to herself for "innocently soliciting the jealousy of others... and knowing just how they must feel." In it she drew striking parallels between the Kennedys and the famous Kung family of modern China before the Reds took over. She also had a strong empathy for the Kennedy family as public figures and took the opportunity to editorialize on the public's responsibility toward brilliant and courageous leadership.

Age did not stop the flow of new books from this remarkable woman whom detractors had long since dubbed "the factory." Her lawyer, Charles M. Solomon, remembered, "She wrote five pages daily and stopped, about 200 words to the printed page. She wrote simply and accurately. In spite of her austerity for saving to aid causes, she did have a definite air of reality, knew how to enjoy an armchair, be received like a queen, which she was in her own way. Her method of writing? She had it already organized in her mind, ordered, even worded."

Solomon enjoyed working with Pearl and related an experience which reflected the more whimsical side of her personality. She was autographing a book for him, and when she asked what his initial "M" stood for, he playfully answered, "Mary." She then wrote on the fly leaf, "To Charles Mary Solomon."

On February 3, 1964, Pearl saw the realization of another dream when the Pearl S. Buck Foundation was incorporated in Delaware. With the names of such prominent celebrities as President Dwight D. Eisenhower, Her Serene Highness the Princess Grace of Monaco and her old friend, actress Joan Crawford, on the new foundation letterhead, she felt ensured of its success.

In her initial letter announcing the new venture, Pearl wrote: "After fifteen years in the field of lost and needy children I am convinced that the most needy in the world are the children born in Asia but whose fathers are American. In all family-oriented societies of Asia such children have little chance of education or jobs. They are considered foreigners and thus ostracized.

"We Americans are partly responsible for them. It is not good for American prestige that our half-American children should grow up illiterate, driven by destitution into criminality and prostitution. But our troops are still there, and so many children continue to be born, about a thousand a year. I plan to spend the rest of my life and strength helping the Korean children right where they are. My foundation will place a permanent representative in Korea to find the half-American ones, and we will try to keep them with their mothers. And we will try to help the mothers find work and make a good home.

"It is my hope that because each of the children is an American, he will be proud of our share in him and be an honor to our efforts on his behalf."

Then followed a strenuous twenty-one city tour across the country to promote and raise money for the new Pearl S. Buck Foundation, with "The Empress," as some of her family called her, the star attraction. Starting in Harrisburg, Pennsylvania, then

The old barn at Green Hills Farms served as the world headquarters of the Pearl S. Buck Foundation from 1964 to 1988. It now serves as the gift shop and reception area for tours. Her home is in the background.

flying on to New Orleans, she faced media interviews and formal dinners—climaxing in one of the soon-to-be famous Good Earth Balls with Pearl leading the dancers in a sprightly waltz. She had learned the useful art of theatrical makeup from Danielewski, so that with her white hair, diamond tiara and priceless Chinese robes, she looked quite regal. It was all a new experience for Pearl S. Buck, and she loved every minute.

Once again she used her tremendous energies and resources for a cause she believed in. She attended every board meeting of the Foundation from 1964 to within one month of her death and poured all her financial resources into the undertaking. She made a gift of seven million dollars to establish the Foundation, the largest single gift ever made by an author for a particular cause. The satisfaction she felt in Foundation work was far greater than the amount of money she had invested.

When Dan Bailey was the Executive Director of the Foundation in the mid-seventies, he made a journey to East Asia to visit some of their Amerasian children's centers. He described one trip as follows: "I have kicked around the world for over 25 years, a lot of it in Asia. I have never had an experience so totally moving. I am not talking about the wars in Vietnam or Korea. I'm talking about going with our caseworkers back into the slums of Asia.

"I was touched many times by the sights never previously seen and the way these youngsters' faces—normally depressed, cheerless, without anything to play with...these faces lit up like a neon sign at the sight of our caseworker.

"I was tremendously impressed with the neighbors and the families living around these children. It was a kind of "open sesame" when the caseworker, who might be four-feet-eleven and weigh less than ninety pounds, should walk in, and a way would sort of clear like the legend of the Red Sea parting.

"I was immediately suspect because I was white and they had never seen me before, but when I was identified with the caseworker, I was welcomed as a friend.

"I was impressed when I was told that some of these places seem so wild to the outsider that the police will not go into them. There are people who are born, live and die in these slums, who never see the outside world at all. They don't have streets as such and there are no telephones or sanitary facilities.

"They have their own remarkable communications system and if a policeman's face shows up even out on the edges of the slums, the word is flashed around even in a few seconds and he wouldn't think of going inside because he fears he might be killed.

"In Bangkok the slums are not located on the ground. There isn't enough ground around for these people to live on so they build flimsy platforms on spindly stilts out over the back waters of the river. These back waters do not flow, they don't even move. They are filled with animal filth, human excrement and every conceivable manner of trash.

"They get in and out of these areas and move about on a board that is very narrow, like catwalks in mine or factory areas. The caseworker walked through as if she had been born to such experience but I was scared to death I might slip and fall. I did once in Bangkok. It caused such a stir that after I was rescued they all gathered to throw very filthy water onto me to wash off the filth I'd fallen into.

"The job that our caseworkers are doing, the reception that they are getting, the respect that they have in the countries they serve, both from the government and the people, is far better and far more effective than any other work being done by any other child care organization in Asia. I say this without any fear of contradiction.

"Now, I had to look at what some of the biggest organizations are doing, an intimate look because when I went back into the slum areas (I was our first executive to venture into the slums, by the way), I was able to make comparisons, and I came out of this with a huge sense of pride, as I indicated to Charles Solomon and Cal Baker. I now know what Senator Mondale was raising so much hell about with the government accounting offices and other agencies. Incidentally, I now understand why they left us out—because we were a clean operation.

"The dedication, the spunk, the raw courage that a thirty-year-old, four-foot-eleven, under-ninety-pounds case worker has in looking after from eighty to one hundred twenty children on a salary of one hundred U.S. dollars a month was a thing that left me with a feeling of humility.

"Now we have problems. Having been there now will help us all straighten out most problems. Miraculously, in terms of doing the job with the children, we are doing far better that I thought we might be. We are definitely doing far better than other organizations. The new efforts we must tackle are more along the lines of physical and mental health.

"There is so much more to do...."

The Final Years

~ CHAPTER 18

At two o'clock in the morning when Pearl was seventy-six, she went to the airport to meet yet another young girl from Korea. Now known as Julie Walsh Henning, the fourteen-year-old girl had been born in Pusan on May 14, 1954. She was impressed that this great lady took the time, effort and pains to personally greet her arrival.

While visiting in Korea the year before, Pearl had been touched by the discrimination against this motherless child and began the year-long effort to bring her to the United States. Pearl took Julie into her own home; she welcomed the chance to mother yet another child. She took Julie to the Philadelphia Symphony and on speaking engagements. She taught her to play chess and provided her with piano lessons. Pearl even attended the Penn Ridge High School PTA meetings. Always she encouraged this late-life child, being loving and supportive as well as giving guidance and advice. She knew from personal experience how difficult it could be to adjust to a new environment. For a teenager in a strange country, Pearl's nurturing support and grandmotherly tolerance were exactly what Julie needed. In turn, the lively teenager gave Pearl the warm companionship and loving support that she needed.

Pearl spent more time than ever reading books and magazines over a wide range of topics including gardening, home life, farming, politics, world affairs, philosophy, psychology, medicine, health—the list was inexhaustible. As she tended her roses and puttered about in the well-tended hothouses, her mind drifted more and more into the remembrances of the past. It was a delight to have an eager listener in the young teenager, and Pearl told Julie the stories of her childhood in China. Although she was a very complicated person, Pearl had always aspired to simplicity. The beauty and order of the Chinese style had assisted her in being less complicated than she might otherwise have been.

Her last great Chinese novel would have a contemporary theme, for *The Three Daughters of Madame Liang* was the story of a Chinese woman with her own restaurant in modern Shanghai and of her three daughters. Pearl made the historical transition from before the Japanese occupation in China to after the Reds took over in less than half a page. "Then they came in, the silent army, grim as the gray tide of the sea. They took possession of everything even to the very soul of man." She bemoaned: "They do not see that even the good and the wise are at the mercy of those who carry the weapon. The old teachings no longer serve, not because they are wrong but because the world around us is barbarian." It was a Book-of-the-Month Club choice, while the *Reader's Digest* bought the condensation rights.

Good Housekeeping readers had voted Pearl S. Buck second in popularity only to Rose Kennedy. She was made a Doctor of Law, Doctor of Letters and Doctor of Humane Letters at various universities.

Pearl often recalled that when she had left her adopted home to live in America, Chinese acquaintances had prophesied that in her old age she would return.

When President Richard Nixon made his memorable trip to China, in which he literally reopened that vast country to the rest of the world, Pearl, then 79 years old, decided that she would follow in his footsteps. The proposed visit was duly announced in the press together with a vast number of writing and media projects connected with the journey. She paid a visit to the Chinese consulate in Canada, applied to Peking for a visa and consulted with the State Department in Washington. Because she had previously announced, "I had been invited to go with the President" and "I know Chou En-lai…a very brilliant man," she expected no opposition to her journey. Pearl was now an old woman, and none more than the Chinese revered the aged. Finally she heard from the Canadian Embassy of the People's Republic of China.

Dear Miss Buck:

Your letters have been duly received. In view of the fact that for a long time you have in your works taken an attitude of distortion, smear and vilification toward the people of new China and its leaders, I am authorized to inform you that we cannot accept your request for a visit to China.

Sincerely yours,

H. L. Yuan

Second Secretary

Never one to dwell on failure, Pearl completed her forty-third novel, *The Rainbow*, while her forty-second, *All Under Heaven*, was awaiting publication. Life in the latter book is depicted as a membrane of days and nights with routines of food, work, sleep and necessities. Yet always and again readers are lifted mentally and spiritually to an intensity they have forgotten. She challenges people to help make the phrase "Under Heaven all men are brothers" come true. "I am only a lonely woman sitting at her desk. I can but give you this book. It is up to you to help make the phrase come true, to complete the title with all its meaning."

Pearl looked forward to her eightieth birthday celebration. Elaborate security systems were installed at Green Hills Farm for the occasion. Daughter Janice and friend Joan also gave a lovely surprise party. Pearl was resplendent in a maroon gown that set off perfectly the white of her hair. Pearl told her faithful housekeeper, Mrs. Galla, that she intended to live to be at least a hundred years old.

Sadly, it proved to be the last birthday she would know, for shortly afterwards her health began to deteriorate rapidly. A painful gallbladder operation was followed by more major surgery. Then she went to her home at Danby, Vermont, hopefully, to recuperate.

When it became apparent that she was sinking fast, Grace made the "long journey" to see Pearl for the last time. She found her older sister sitting straight-backed in an armchair, reminiscent of that last great Empress of China, about whose life Pearl had written in *Imperial Woman*. In her red and black Chinese gown, long red earrings and necklace to match, a clear-minded Pearl S. Buck was still in full command of the situation.

Pearl died during the morning hours of March 6, 1973.

Pearl Buck at her 80th birthday party, June 26, 1972.

Pearl's final resting place at the Farm with her name written in Chinese characters. Her grave has been visited by thousands of people from all over the world.

The funeral was held at Green Hills Farm with a little service in the library, where she had enjoyed so many happy times with her beloved Richard. Mrs. Galla crocheted a blue and white afghan as a coverlet for Pearl, who lay dressed in a white Chinese robe in her casket. The adopted children had brought along the fourteen grandchildren, who were all taken to see their famous grandmother lying in state.

She was laid to rest under the big ash tree just below the farmhouse and barn near the road. Her grave was surrounded by a low railing and marked by a simple marble stone carved with the Chinese characters for her name. It was the embodiment of the beauty and order after which she patterned her life.

In a fitting obituary on March 7, 1973, *New York Times* writer Albin Krebs eulogized, "She lived a long life as artist, wife, mother and philanthropist."

Pearl would have liked that.

The *San Francisco Chronicle* reported: "In Washington, President Nixon described Miss Buck as a 'human bridge between the civilization of the East and the West.' Her writings had enabled millions to see the beauty of China and its people at a time when direct personal contact was all but impossible."

No person in human history has ever written of another country and another race as voluminously, deeply, richly as Pearl Buck did of China. Not only did she influence the entire world with her written works, which have been translated into 58 different languages, but she continues to influence current and future generations through her writings, which are still popular, and through the philanthropies she established to help Amerasian children.

Vachel Lindsay's words best describe the immortality   **185**
Pearl Buck deserves.

> Sleep on, O brave hearted…that kindled the flame—
> To live in mankind is far more than to live in a name
> To live in mankind, far, far more…than to live in a name.

Epilogue

❧

In the years I have been lecturing about Pearl Buck, I have always been asked about her views and ideas. I've tried to reveal them for this book by carefully selecting excerpts from her writings and conversations.

But Pearl Buck was a very private person and seldom let anyone into the world of her mind. She once shared with some of us the following thoughts: "I really seldom care to go visiting. I'd rather stay at home. When I'm invited somewhere, I try to leave as much of myself here at home as possible. I do not take my problems with me."

Her preference when visiting was to be told what time meals were to be served. She wanted her hosts to be themselves. She preferred not to be asked about herself. She wished to be as inconspicuous as possible and savor all she could of the family she was visiting.

She spoke always of "temporarily." While on a visit she was living away from home "temporarily," so she would enjoy their kindness, generosity and sharing: "I may see new pictures, new scenes and hear new thoughts. I am temporarily diverted, cheered and inspired. When I return home I have new gifts of memory, new sights to remember and new voices to recall. I have taken what I need on the journey but not my whole self. I leave to my own home as much as possible of myself."

She had her own favorite foods and enjoyments but could accommodate herself happily to other people's tastes as long as she knew it was only temporary. Although she liked to go to bed early, she could stay up late if she was having a good time. She said, "I am amused by almost anything—temporarily—even the silliest game."

These comments reveal a great deal about her desire for privacy.

I have often returned to the scenes of my years of working for Pearl. My experiences took me from coast to coast.

While driving to Green Hills Farm, I recalled the day she had given me directions. I was to travel on a particular road near Dublin in Bucks County, Pennsylvania, until I came to a three-arched bridge. She didn't realize that the arches were under the bridge and couldn't be seen from the road. I went back and forth over many bridges until I finally located the right one.

The trees she and Richard had planted at the Farm are mature now, and the site is so wooded that the house and barn can scarcely be seen in passing. The farm is now a national historic landmark, but I can still feel her spirit in its comfortable rooms and almost hear the happy cries of the many children they raised.

I revisited the Geary Theater in San Francisco where, through the arrangements of the Association, Uday Shankar was presenting his movie *Kalpana*. Kalpana means imagination.

Behind the scenes it was near chaos because of a strike. When the multi-reel film was delivered in a heavy old trunk to the theater lobby, we could not get anyone to help us carry the film up to the projectionist's booth, which seemed to be at least five stories high—and had no elevator to serve us. The three of us—Mr. Shankar, the Consul General of India in San Francisco and I—somehow lugged the heavy load to the upper regions of the theater and the evening began.

The movie played to a full house. They even had to turn people away at the door, and everyone thought it was a huge success.

At the end of the showing, we couldn't find anyone to help us with the return trip. Just at that moment, the last person leaving turned off all the lights! We had to descend the stairs in utter darkness from that same projection booth with those twenty-some reels. How we made it down those dark stairs without breaking our necks I'll never know! It seemed like hours until the three of us replaced all the reels in the trunk and transported them to the Consul General's apartment. It was a great night, a triumph for East and West and our aching backs. Over a midnight supper, Mr. Shankar chided, "And you people remark about primitive India!"

I revisited Columbia University where, as Pearl's personal representative, I had been present when General Eisenhower, President of Columbia at that time, gave Nehru an honorary Doctor of Law at the Columbia Law Memorial Library. I still remember the citation for Nehru: "...the foremost disciple of the great apostle of Indian freedom (Gandhi), indomitable leader of his people along the thorny path of liberation, wise counselor and molder of policies of a reborn nation."

I was present at the heart-rending reunion of a little Amerasian girl with her black father, featured on all the major television networks. I met them again later when he brought her, his American children and his wife to the unveiling of the Pearl Buck Commemorative Postage Stamp at Green Hills Farm in May 1982. I knew Pearl would be happy that more and more American fathers are attempting to bring their Amerasian offspring to the United States and incorporate them into their American families.

Mary G. Roebling, Chairman Emeritus of the National State Bank in Trenton, New Jersey, shared with me her reminiscences of Pearl Buck as she had known her.

"When I first met Pearl Buck I was struck, instantly, by what I called her four Gigantics: her gigantic strength and self-discipline; her gigantic sensitivity and gentleness; her gigantic sense of humor; and her gigantic intellectualism and skill.

"After only a few moments of conversation with Pearl Buck I knew why she had won the Nobel Prize for Literature. She had mastered herself. She had mastered all of the many skills given her at birth, and she had succeeded in deriving from each the maximal productivity. She was fully in charge of Pearl Sydenstricker Buck Walsh, and being in charge she could acquire and develop new aptitudes, crafts and arts.

"Pearl's sensitivity and gentleness were plain for all to see. Yet in no way was she a shy flower. She could be a fighter, and she never hesitated to speak out against, or to write against, things she considered wrong.... In 1940, she stated forcefully her belief in equal rights for women, even before America's attitude toward women began to change as a result of World War II. This was the move of a courageous and tough-minded woman.

On the grounds of Green Hills Farm, the author at the unveiling of the Pearl Buck Commemorative stamp in 1982. The childrens' playhouse and part of the barn are in the background.

"Yet her compassion for other people, especially children, especially children in need, was more pervasive.

"Pearl Buck's sense of humor was a marvelous thing to behold. I believe that in her self-mastery she had learned that a person's problems are only so big as he or she lets them be and that, basically, she was a happy and fulfilled woman. This reinforced the fundamentally happy outlook she had toward life, permitting her to see the absurd comedy in so many of mankind's endeavors and permitting her to laugh at them, even as she laughed often at her own pursuits, such as when the Kansas City high schools barred *The Good Earth* from their libraries in 1935....

"I personally do not think the world has yet fully realized the depth and complexity of Pearl Buck's genius. I believe that in time to come the better universities will offer special studies on this mental giant and on her works, not only as a writer but as a citizen. In scores of essays she demonstrated her profound conviction that citizens of a democracy have an inescapable responsibility to speak out on and to act on issues of public importance.

"It was not the sheer prodigiousness of Pearl Buck's writings that made her great, of course, but the exciting and satisfying lore they contained. In nearly every book, article, essay and short story there is a pronounced or underlying theme of love, because Pearl Buck was in love with the world and all its peoples, and she made our lives richer by telling us about her feelings and the feelings of mankind. Our debt to her is unending."

As I travelled for Pearl, I was thunderstruck at the influence her book *The Good Earth* had on people's lives. I came across instances of her influence time and time again. I talked with a soldier in Pittsburgh who, from reading the book, determined to go to Israel if he survived World War II. While there, he met and married a woman at an Israeli university. They are both now working in Israel, but doing humanitarian work on both sides of the Atlantic, all because of the inspiration of Pearl Buck.

I found that Pearl Buck was first in the hearts of good men and good women the world around. Nobel prize winner, humanitarian, gracious lady, honored mother—not only to her own, but to countless thousands from World War II, the Korean War and the Vietnam War—beloved wife, keen American, this is Pearl S. Buck as I knew her.

In 1978 I read an Associated Press announcement that stated, "Pearl Buck wrote over 65 novels, the first of which was not published until she was 38." I have seen estimates from sixty-five all the way to ninety. That she was prolific with her works, there is no doubt. The number of her novels depends on how her works are categorized. Some divide her works into fiction, general and juvenile. Others divide them into fiction and nonfiction, mixing juvenile and adult. Still others divide them into fiction, biographies, general and short stories. Some of her works have been published posthumously. I include the list compiled by the Pearl S. Buck Foundation in the back of this book for you to make your own judgements.

In writing *Good Earth Mother,* I talked to many people who had known or been influenced by Pearl Buck. I reread the letters she had written to me and pondered the many philosophical conversations I had enjoyed with her and Richard Walsh. In doing so, I realized that no one would ever be able to capture the essence of this great lady, who had such a tremendous influence on my life.

194   As I visited her grave on the fourteenth anniversary of her death, I placed a single red rose by the gravestone and paraphrased Mary Roebling's words, "My debt to you is unending."

Welcome House and
the Pearl S. Buck Foundation Today

At the time of its founding, Welcome House was unique in the entire world for mixed-blood adoption. At first there were more interested families than available children, but this changed radically after the Korean and Vietnam Wars. Today, in an average year, Welcome House oversees the adoption of 250 children and is able to operate profitably. It has become so famous that it even has a road named for it, which one sees when one visits Green Hills Farm.

In the first ten years that Welcome House was in existence, more than one hundred babies were placed in adoptive homes throughout the United States. Welcome House made an effort to adopt as many of the Amerasian children as possible, but for those who could not come to America for adoption, it acted as a group of Americans interested in their welfare. This facet of Welcome House eventually was taken over by the Pearl S. Buck Foundation.

For those children adopted by American families, Welcome House acted as a force to change the outlook of the community, not by compulsion, but by enlargement. As the hearts of people were touched naturally and easily through the presence in their community of these lovely half-Asian children, the minds of people were enlarged to wonder about the Asian lands, to inquire and to learn. Through these children, the countries they used to call foreign were no longer distant to them. It was not strange to include China and Japan in their national heritage.

Once a year as many as possible of the adoptive families meet to renew their friendship, show off the children and discuss possible problems in family and community. A cooperating psychologist, joining the adoptive parents in special sessions, has remarked that the problems are simple and normal, seldom related to the mixed blood of the children. This means that when a mixed-blood child is placed in a family that approves of him and sees only advantage in his birth, the community follows. Welcome House is careful that the children go to such a family.

Although the original Welcome House building is no longer there, the agency still exists as an accredited placement service with a full-time social worker.

The unchanging insistence of Welcome House that the happiness of the child is the most important goal for its work rather than the propagation of racial or religious origins has helped to broaden the placement policy of other agencies. Some of them, which in the past never accepted mixed-blood children because they could not find mixed-blood parents, are now accepting these children and placing them with warmhearted families regardless of race and religion. The best family for a special child would hopefully include similar racial and religious ancestry, but not necessarily. Certainly no child should be kept an orphan because these nonessentials cannot be matched. The only true essential is love and complete acceptance of the child as he or she is.

The *New York Daily News* on Monday, April 23, 1979, featured an article which began, "PEARL BUCK STILL LIVES." It must have startled those who remembered her death in March 1973. The article which followed was written about the celebration of the fifteenth anniversary of the founding of the Pearl S. Buck Foundation. Hundreds of sponsors, friends, ambassadors and U.N. personnel gathered at the Plaza Hotel to celebrate Pearl Buck's dream to help the

Amerasian children through a foundation. Among the Advisory Board of Governors attending were Arlene Dahl, Carol and Dom DeLuise, Robert Vaughn, Jean Stapleton, Dr. Christiaan Barnard (who had traveled from South Africa to deliver the main address) and this author. It was unforgettable.

Beverly Sills was honored that day as the first woman recipient of the Pearl Buck Woman of the Year award, She received an original piece of sculpture by Madeline Smith, a personal friend of Pearl Buck. Miss Sills was selected by a panel of judges that included Hedley Donovan of *Time* magazine, Edward Thompson of *Reader's Digest,* John Hughes of the *Christian Science Monitor,* James Hoge of the *Chicago Sun Times,* Tom Simmons of the *Dallas Morning Herald,* and Lenore Hersey of the *Ladies Home Journal.*

Dr. Barnard remarked, "What is most important after a traumatic experience is not what you have lost but what use you make of what is left. It is our duty to these children who have lost something to help them make the most of what is left" after their fathers abandoned them. In some cases Asian relatives also abandoned them. *Insight,* the quarterly publication of the Pearl Buck Foundation, said of Dr. Barnard's speech, "The Surgeon with the Open Heart operated on all our hearts."

Each year since then the Foundation has chosen a Pearl Buck Woman of the Year. Recipients have included Lois Burpee, Erma Bombeck, Carol Arthur DeLuise, Sally Jesse Raphael and a nun from New Jersey who received the award for her special work with children.

With every passing year more children have been born to our servicemen or business and professional men stationed overseas. The Foundation has increased the number of children under its care from a few thousand to over seven thousand per year. Even with the Foundation spearheading the return from Vietnam of many children, tens of thousands are still roaming the streets of Asian cities—destitute, lonely and forgotten. The Pearl Buck Foundation persists in assisting these children. The work of the Foundation has been featured by Hugh Downs on ABC television, on CBS's "Sixty Minutes" and by NBC's David Brinkley. The evening news often featured John Shade, former

Executive Director, when the Foundation was aiding the return of many children from Vietnam.

On November 17, 1981, Shade appeared before the House Judiciary SubCommittee on Immigration, Refugees and International Law. The occasion was to hear testimony on H.R. 008 regarding the welfare of Amerasian children. Shade said: "When the father is absent in Asia, which is almost always the case with Amerasians, the key to life in Asia, and all its aspects of socialization and acculturation, as well as general societal acceptance, is missing. The father is the key to birth registration, legitimacy, citizenship, education, employment and marriage. Without some substitute or advocate there are often problems which simply cannot be overcome. The Amerasian as a class is analogous to those who may share his/her low socio-economic profile or certain deprivations. There are none whose day to day survival is either so convoluted or so uncertain; there are none, who by their birthright, have the potential for so much and have been given so little.

"The Amerasian children exist in a political limbo where citizenship is in question in more than one country where they are found, and the basic rights of the child are denied. The U.N. in 1950 began to outline the basic rights of all children. By 1959 they had listed such basic rights. It is precisely these rights which the Amerasian children are often denied. What are these right as outlined by the U.N.?

1. The right to affection, love and understanding.
2. The right to adequate nutrition and medical care.
3. The right to free education.
4. The right to full opportunity for play and recreation.
5. The right to name and nationality.
6. The right to special care if handicapped.
7. The right to be among the first to receive relief in times of disaster.
8. The right to be a useful member of society and to develop individual abilities.
9. The right to be brought up in peace.
10. The right to enjoy these rights, regardless of race, color, sex, religion, national or social origin.

"Since the turn of the century the United States has visited hundreds of thousands of these Amerasian children upon already overcrowded agrarian populations of Asia.... At the very same time we have stressed population control among indigenous people, we have added to their burdens.... The Asian seems unable to cope with the Amerasian problem; the Americans have found it exceedingly difficult to develop policies with this uncomfortable and unwieldy human rights issue."

He testified again on June 21, 1983, at a special Congressional Hearing specifically on the Amerasians. Both appearances were brief, direct, well-prepared and ably rendered.

Since 1982 the Foundation has concentrated its efforts on five major countries: Korea, Okinawa, Taiwan, the Philippines and Thailand— with the heaviest emphasis upon the last two.

In the spring of 1986 the Foundation broke ground to open the new International Headquarters beside the parking lot at Green Hills Farm. The barn has been used all these years as the inadequate offices while Amerasians have grown from a few hundred to over 9500. The new offices were dedicated in April 1988.

The Foundation operates with the money from sponsors combined with royalty money from Pearl Buck's books and other fund raising monies to make possible the ongoing assistance. Of the $24 per month sponsorship fee, all but $1.80 goes for direct child support. The Foundation does not use money for overseas community projects or paid ads. When you see Advisory Governors Jean Stapleton or Robert Vaughn in an ad on television, they are doing it without compensation.

The Pearl Buck Foundation sponsorship program is the only program anywhere that provides direct cash support to the child and his family through social workers in the Asian countries. It is the only sponsorship operating on an international basis. In Korea, where there are other adoption agencies for Amerasian children, the Pearl Buck Foundation budget exceeds all the others added together. Dollar for dollar, soul for soul, no other agency, individual or government has done more for the Amerasian child than the Pearl Buck Foundation.

A sponsor writes to and receives letters from the child being sponsored; he also receives annual pictures of the child. The correspondence is monitored to protect both the sponsor and the child. Letters are true originals from the children themselves with translations provided by volunteers where necessary. The sponsor helps the child understand and value his American background.

Here is but a portion of a letter from a Japanese girl given partial support for twelve years. Upon finishing college, she wrote, "I almost gave up many times, but you people were always with me and encouraged me and supported me way beyond the ordinary material things. I thank you for your moral and financial support. I read everything I could about Pearl Buck. From now on I will try to be like her and love people and live peacefully in the world. I will never forget your kindnesses all my life. Sincerely, Aiko."

In the fall of 1991 the Boards of Directors of Welcome House and the Foundation were merged. Any information about either of these philanthropies is available from the headquarters of the Foundation at Green Hills Farm, Bucks County, Perkasie, PA, 18944. Although any gift, large or small, is welcome, the most important key to all Foundation services is to be a sponsor.

The Works of Pearl S. Buck

⪥ BIBLIOGRAPHY

N ot only was Pearl Buck a prolific writer, but her works were often included as excerpts or in toto in her own and other publications. To keep this list to a manageable length I have excluded excerpts, publications other than the first appearance, and publications in other countries and languages. Items are listed by the name first used for publication. When the name was changed for another publication, the new name appears in parentheses.

This task proved to be almost insurmountable as the *Reader's Guide to Periodical Literature* in the 1930s and 1940s did not include *Cosmopolitan, Family Week, Opportunity, Redbook, This Week* and other magazines to which she sold stories and articles. I had an invaluable source in Lee Rudisill of Philomath, Oregon who has the most extensive private collection of Pearl Buck's works that I have seen. I found additional references to short stories in the lists of "Outstanding Short Stories" in the series *Short Story Index* and *Best American Short Stories* for the applicable years and references to nonfiction articles in the *Essays and General Literature Index* and the *Education Index*.

Most of the books were either in my own library, Lee Rudisill's library or in public and university libraries. Where I couldn't find an original source I used Lucille S. Zinn's list "The Works of Pearl S. Buck: A Bibliography" from the *Bulletin of Bibliography, Vol. 36, No. 4* for corroboration.

NOVELS AND NOVELLAS

Magazine names indicate that the novel or novella first appeared as a serialization in that magazine. Those which never made it into book form in this country are indicated with an asterisk (*).

All Men Are Brothers, 1933; translated from Chinese by PSB
All Under Heaven, 1973; posthumous
An American Legend (Other Gods, An American Legend), 1939;
    Good Housekeeping
The Angry Wife, 1947; John Sedges pseudonym
Bright Procession, 1952; John Sedges pseudonym
China Flight, 1942; *Collier's*
* "China Gold," 1942; *Collier's*
China Sky, 1941; *Collier's*
Come, My Beloved, 1953
Command the Morning, 1959
Death in the Castle, 1965
Dragon Seed, 1942; *Asia*
East Wind: West Wind, 1930; *Asia* & *Collier's*
The Goddess Abides, 1972
God's Men, 1951; *Woman's Home Companion*
The Good Earth, 1931; Pulitzer Prize winner
The Hidden Flower, 1952; *Woman's Home Companion*
A House Divided, 1935
Imperial Woman, 1956; *Woman's Home Companion*
Kinfolk, 1949; *Ladies Home Journal*
Letter from Peking, 1957
The Living Reed, 1963
The Long Love, 1949; John Sedges pseudonym
Mandala, 1970

A Man's Daily Bread (*Portrait of a Marriage*), 1941; *Redbook*   **203**
The Mother, 1933; *Cosmopolitan*
The New Year, 1968
* "No Time for Love," 1951; *Redbook*
* "Now and Forever," 1937; *Woman's Home Companion*
The Patriot, 1939
Pavilion of Women, 1946; *Woman's Home Companion*
Peony, 1948
The Promise, 1943; *Asia*
The Rainbow, 1974; posthumous
* "The Real Thing," 1944; *Cosmopolitan*
Satan Never Sleeps, 1962
Sons, 1932; *Cosmopolitan*
This Proud Heart, 1938; *Good Housekeeping*
The Three Daughters of Madame Liang, 1969
The Time Is Noon, 1966
The Townsman, 1945; John Sedges pseudonym
Voices in the House, 1953; John Sedges pseudonym

SHORT STORIES

The intials PSB indicate anthologies composed entirely of Pearl S. Buck's stories.

"All the Days of Love and Courage" ("The Christmas Child"), 1969;
    Good Housekeeping
"The Angel," 1937; *Woman's Home Companion*
"Barren Spring," 1932; *Spectator*
"Beautiful Ladies," 1934; *Collier's*
"The Beauty," 1961; *Ladies Home Journal*
"Begin to Live," 1945; *Woman's Home Companion*
"Between These Two," 1935; *Cosmopolitan*
"Beyond Language;" PSB, *Fourteen Stories*
"By the Hand of a Child," 1911; *Helianthus*
"The Castle;" PSB, *The Woman Who Was Changed and Other Stories*
"A Chinese Woman Speaks" (became *East Wind: West Wind*), 1926; *Asia*
"Christmas Away from Home;" PSB, *Once upon a Christmas*
"The Christmas Child;" PSB, *Once upon a Christmas*

204

"Christmas Day in the Morning," 1955; *Collier's*

"The Christmas Scent;" PSB, *Once upon a Christmas*

"Christmas Verities;" PSB, *Once upon a Christmas*

"The Cockfight;" PSB, *The Good Deed and Other Stories of Asia Past and Present*

"The Commander and the Commissar;" PSB, *Fourteen Stories*

"The Communist;" PSB, *The First Wife and Other Stories*

"Conqueror's Girl;" Singer, K., *Famous Short Stories, vol.1*

"The Courtyards of Peace;" PSB, *The Good Deed and Other Stories of Asia Past and Present*

"The Crusade," 1936; *Scribners*

"Dagger in the Dark;" PSB, *The Good Deed and Other Stories of Asia Past and Present*

"The Dance," 1935; *Collier's*

"Death and the Dawn," 1956; *Ladies Home Journal*

"Dream Child;" PSB, *East and West*

"Duet in Asia;" PSB, *The Good Deed and Other Stories of Asia Past and Present*

"Enchantment;" PSB, *Fourteen Stories*

"The Enemy," 1942; *Harpers;* O. Henry Award

"The Engagement;" PSB, *Fourteen Stories*

"Enough for a Lifetime," 1935; *Woman's Home Companion*

"The Face of Buddha;" PSB, *Today and Forever, Stories of China*

"Face of Gold," 1940; *Saturday Evening Post*

"Faithfully Yours," 1947; *Redbook*

"Father Andrea," 1929; *Asia*

"Fathers and Mothers;" PSB, *The First Wife and Other Stories*

"A Few People;" PSB, *Far and Near: Stories of China, Japan and America*

"A Field of Rice," 1962; *Saturday Evening Post*

"The First Wife," 1932; *Asia*

"Fool's Sacrifice," 1934; *Cosmopolitan*

"Francesca," 1948; *Good Housekeeping*

"The Frill," 1933; *Woman's Home Companion;* O. Henry Award

"Gift of Laughter," 1943; *American Magazine*

"Gifts of Joy," 1971; *Good Housekeeping*

"Going Home;" PSB, *The Good Deed and Other Stories of Asia Past and Present*

"The Golden Bowl;" PSB, *East and West*   **205**
"Golden Flower," 1940; *Woman's Home Companion*
"The Good River;" PSB, *The First Wife and Other Stories*
"Guerilla Mother;" PSB, *Today and Forever, Stories of China*
"Hearts Come Home," 1935; *Ladies Home Journal*
"Heat Wave," 1935; *American Mercury*
"Here and Now;" PSB, *Secrets of the Heart*
"Hidden Is the Golden Dragon," 1933; *Asia*
"His Own Country," 1935; *Cosmopolitan*
"Home Girl;" PSB, *Far and Near: Stories of China, Japan and America*
"Home to Heaven;" PSB, *Far and Near: Stories of China, Japan and America*
"Hour of Worship," 1911; *The Tattler*
"A Husband for Lili" ("The Good Deed"), 1953; *Woman's Home Companion*
"If It Must Be So," PSB, *The Woman Who Was Changed and Other Stories*
"Incident at Wang's Corner," 1947; *This Week*
"India, India," 1964; *McCalls*
"In Loving Memory," 1972; *Good Housekeeping*
"John-John Chinaman," 1942; *American Magazine*
"Journey for Life," 1944; *American Magazine*
"The Kiss;" PSB, *The Lovers and Other Stories*
"Ko-Sen the Sacrificed," 1937; *Champ*
"The Lesson;" PSB, *Today and Forever, Stories of China*
"Letter from India;" PSB, *East and West*
"Letter Home;" PSB, *The Good Deed and Other Stories of Asia Past and Present*
"Little Red;" McHargue, G., comp., *The Best of Both Worlds*
"The Lovers;" PSB, *The Lovers and Other Stories*
"A Man's Foes;" PSB, *Today and Forever, Stories of China*
"Melissa," 1960; *Good Housekeeping*
"The Miracle Child," 1973; *Good Housekeeping*
"Miranda;" PSB, *The Lovers and Other Stories*
"Moon over Manhattan," 1953; *McCalls*
"More Than a Woman," 1941; *Good Housekeeping*
"Morning in the Park;" PSB, *Secrets of the Heart*
"Mother and Sons;" PSB, *Far and Near: Stories of China, Japan and America*
"Mr. Binney's Afternoon," 1935; *Dick*
"Mr. Right;" PSB, *Far and Near: Stories of China, Japan and America*

"Mrs. Barton Declines," 1973; *Ladies Home Journal*

"Mrs. Mercer and Her Self;" PSB, *Far and Near: Stories of China, Japan and America*

"Mrs. Starling's Problem," 1974; *Ladies Home Journal;* posthumous

"The New Christmas;" PSB, *Once upon a Christmas*

"The New Road," 1930; *Asia*

"Next Saturday and Forever;" PSB, *The Lovers and Other Stories*

"No Other Gods," 1936; *Pictorial Review*

"No Room at the Inn;" PSB, *Once upon a Christmas*

"The Old Chinese Nurse," 1932; *Fortnightly* & *Country Gentleman*

"The Old Demon," 1939; *Cosmopolitan*

"The Old Mother;" PSB, *The First Wife and Other Stories*

"Old Signs Fail," 1940; *Woman's Home Companion*

"Once upon a Christmas;" PSB, *Once upon a Christmas*

"One Named Jesus;" Brentano, F., ed., *The Word Lives On*

"The One Woman;" PSB, *Far and Near: Stories of China, Japan and America*

"Parable of Plain People;" PSB, *Fourteen Stories*

"Pleasant Evening;" PSB, *The Woman Who Was Changed and Other Stories*

"The Quarrel," 1932; *Ladies Home Journal*

"The Rainy Day;" PSB, *The First Wife and Other Stories*

"Ransom," 1938; *Cosmopolitan*

"The Refugees;" PSB, *The First Wife and Other Stories*

"Repatriated," 1933; *Redbook*

"The Return," 1933; *Cosmopolitan*

"Revolutionist" ("Wang Lung"), 1928; *Asia*

"The Sacred Skull," 1963; *Saturday Evening Post*

"The Secret of Everything" ("Johnny Jack and His Beginnings"), 1954; *McCalls*

"Secrets of the Heart," 1968; *Good Housekeeping*

"Shanghai Scene," 1934; *Asia*; O. Henry Award

"Shield of Love," 1954; *Collier's*

"The Silver Butterfly," 1960; *Saturday Evening Post*

"Singing to Her Death," 1930; *Asia*

"The Solitary Priest," 1926; *Asia*

"Stranger, Come Home," 1967; *Good Housekeeping*

"Sunrise at Juhu;" PSB, *The Good Deed and Other Stories of Asia Past and Present*

"The Tax Collector;" PSB, *Far and Near: Stories of China, Japan and America*   **207**
"There Was No Peace," 1940; *Collier's*
"This Day to Treasure" ("A Grandmother's Christmas"), 1972; *Good Housekeeping*
"Thoughts of a Woman at Christmas;" PSB, *Once upon a Christmas*
"Tiger! Tiger!," 1938; *Cosmopolitan*
"A Time to Love," 1944; *Ladies Home Journal*
"To Whom a Child Is Born;" PSB, *East and West*
"The Truce," 1936; *Redbook*
"Two in Love," 1970; *Good Housekeeping*
"The Two Women," 1933; *Woman's Home Companion*
"Until Tomorrow;" PSB, *East and West*
"Unwritten Rules," 1953; *Collier's*
"Valley by the Sea," 1911; *The Tattler*
"Vignette of Love" ("Next Saturday and Forever"), 1935; *This Week*
"Virgin Birth;" PSB, *Far and Near: Stories of China, Japan and America*
"The Wandering Little God," 1928; *Asia*
"Wedding and Funeral," 1934; Van Doren, C.C., ed., *Modern American Prose*
"What the Heart Must" ("Someone to Remember"), 1937; *Woman's Home Companion*
"With a Delicate Air," 1961; PSB, *Fourteen Stories*
"Woman in the Waves," 1976; PSB, *Secrets of the Heart*
"The Woman Who Was Changed," 1947; *Redbook*

POETRY

"An Eastern Lullaby;" *The Tattler*
"Song of the Sea;" *The Tattler*
Words of Love, 1974; posthumous

NONFICTION BOOKS AND MONOGRAPHS

American Argument: with Eslanda Goode Robeson, 1949
A Bridge for Passing, 1961; *Ladies Home Journal*
The Child Who Never Grew, 1950
Children for Adoption, 1964
China in Black and White, 1945
China Past and Present, 1972

The Chinese Novel, 1939; Nobel lecture

A Community Success Story: The Founding of the Pearl Buck Center, 1972

The Delights of Learning, 1960; Honors Address

The Exile, 1936; *Woman's Home Companion*

Fighting Angel: Portrait of a Soul, 1936

For Spacious Skies: Journey in Dialogue with Theodore F. Harris, 1966

Friend to Friend: A candid Exchange Between Pearl Buck and Carlos P. Romulo, 1958

The Gifts They Bring: Our Debt to the Mentally Retarded, 1965

How It Happens: Talk about the German People, 1914-1933 with Erna von Pustau, 1947

The Joy of Children, 1964

The Kennedy Women, 1970

My Several Worlds; A Personal Record, 1954

Of Men and Women, 1941

Pearl S. Buck's America, 1971

Pearl S. Buck's Oriental Cookbook, 1972

The People of Japan, 1966

The Story Bible: Volumes I and II, 1971

"Talks with Masha" *(Talk about Russia: With Masha Scott)*, 1945; *Asia and the Americas*

Tell the People: Talks with James Yen about the Mass Education Movement, 1945

NONFICTION ARTICLES

"Advice to Unborn Novelists," 1935; *Saturday Review of Literature*

"Alice Nash," 1950; *Training School Bulletin*

"America's Gunpowder Women," 1939; *Harper's*

"America's Medieval Women," 1938; *Harper's*

"American Imperialism in the Making," 1945; *Asia and the Americas*

"An American Looks at America," 1937; *Opportunity*

"Americans in Distress," 1947; *United Nations World*

"Appeal to California," 1944; *Asia and the Americas*

"Arms for China's Democracy," 1938; *Asia*

"An Artist in a World of Science," 1958; *Saturday Review*

"At Home in the World," 1942; Gruenberg, S.M., ed., *Family in a World at War*

"At Home with Pearl Buck," 1965; *Ladies Home Journal*

"The Atmosphere of Education," 1948; *NEA Journal*   **209**
"Beauty in China," 1924; *Forum*
"The Bomb: Did We Have to Drop It?," 1959; *Readers Digest*
"Books about Americans for People in Asia to Read," 1942; *Asia*
"Breaking the Barriers of Race Prejudice," 1942; *Journal of Negro Education*
"Can England Trust Us?," 1943; *New York Times Magazine*
"Can the Church Be Religious?," 1943; *Christian Century*
"Can the Church Lead?;" PSB, *What America Means to Me*
"A Center of New Life," 1943; *American Journal of Nursing*
"A Certain Star," 1957; *American Weekly*
"Child from Nowhere," 1962; *Ladies Home Journal*
"The Children America Forgot," 1967; *Readers Digest*
"Children Are What You Make Them," 1936; *Forum*
"The Children Waiting. The Shocking Scandal of Adoption" ("Must We
      Have Orphanages?"), 1955; *Woman's Home Companion*
"Children's Crusade for Children;" *Parents Magazine*
"China Against Japan," 1936; *Asia*
"China and the Foreign Chinese," 1932; *Yale Review*
"China and the West," 1933; *Annals of the American Academy*, (Manuscript
      received Cornell's Laura L. Messenger Memorial Prize in 1926.)
"The China Front and the Future of Asia: Controversial Viewpoints,"
      1943; PSB et al., *Amerasia*
"China Lost and Found," 1972; *National PTA Magazine*
"China: Still the Good Earth," 1949; *Saturday Review of Literature*
"China the Eternal," 1924; *International Review of Missions*
"China to America," 1944; Oboler, Arch, *Free World Theater*
"Chinese Attitude Toward Graft" ("Wise Chinese"), 1935; *Harpers*
"Chinese Literature in Today's World," 1946; MacNair, H.F.ed., *China*
"The Chinese Student Mind," 1924; *Nation*
"Chinese War Lords," 1933; *Saturday Evening Post*
"Chinese Women," 1931; *Pacific Affairs*
"Come in, Mary," 1965; *This Week*
"Communism in China," 1928; *Nation*
"Conclusion: East and West," 1945; Christy, A.E.,ed., *Asian Legacy and
      American Life*
"Conflict and Cooperation Across the Pacific Today," 1935; *Opportunity*

"Creative Spirit in Modern China," 1934; *Asia*

"The Darkest Hour in China's History," 1944; *New York Times Magazine*

"Debt to Dickens," 1936; *Saturday Review of Literature*

"Does World Government Mean More Government?," 1947; *United Nations World*

"Don't Throw Away the Best Part," 1942; *Collier's*

"Do You Want Your Children to Be Tolerant?," 1947; *Better Homes and Gardens*

"A Dream for Danby," 1971; *Yankee Magazine*

"The Early Chinese Novel," 1931; *Saturday Review of Literature*

"East and West," 1945; *American Mercury*

"Easter 1933," 1933; *Cosmopolitan*

"Education for Victory," 1944; *Nebraska Educational Journal*

"The Elementary Teacher Is a Champion of the Less Fortunate Child," 1952; *Instructor*

"Elements of Democracy in the Chinese Culture," 1969; *St. John's University*

"The Emotional Chinese," 1926; *Trans-Pacific*

"The Emotional Nature of the Chinese," 1926; *Nation*

"Essay on Life," 1971; *Modern Maturity*

"The Exile's Gift," 1940; *Saturday Review of Literature*

"Fiction and the Front Page," 1936; *Yale Review*

"Fifty Years in the Training School is an Honorable Record," 1948; *Training School Bulletin*

"Films for Neighbors," 1950; *Saturday Review of Literature*

"Food for China," 1947; *Survey Graphic*

"For a People's Peace," 1942; *Progressive Education*

"Foreigners Under Fire," 1937; *Asia*

"Free China Gets to Work," 1939; *Asia*

"Freedom, East and West," 1942; *Common Sense*

"Freedom for All" ("The Heart of Democracy"), 1941; *New York Times*

"Freedom for India Now!," 1941; *Post War World Council*

"The Freedom to Be Free," 1943; *New York Times Magazine*

"Friendly Homes of Bucks County," 1961; *American Home*

"Friends and Enemies of China," 1936; *Asia*

"The Future of the White Man in the Far East," 1940; *Foreign Affairs*

"The Giants Are Gone," 1936; *Asia*

"God Becomes a Convenience," 1936; *Forum*

"The Good People of Japan," 1949; *United Nations World*

"He Who Lives, Wins," 1939; *Asia*

"A Higher Nationalism," 1933; *World Tomorrow*

"The Historic Basis of Friendship," 1971; *Current*

"How I Feel about America," 1970; *Pittsburgh Press*

"I Am the Better Woman for Having My Two Black Children," 1972;
    Today's Health

"In China, Too," 1923; *Atlantic Monthly*

"In Search of a New Book," 1935; *Wilson Bulletin*

"In Search of Readers," 1950, Hull, H.R., ed., *Writer's Book*

"In Search of Teachers," 1956; *Schoolman's Week Proc.*

"Insecurity Breeds Hatred," 1945; *Labor Report*

"Interview with My Adopted Daughter," 1946; *Readers Digest*

"Introduction," 1935; Lin Yutang, *My Country and My People*

"Introduction to the United States," 1939; *Saturday Review of Literature*

"Is There a Case for Foreign Missions?," 1933; *Harpers*

"It Takes Courage," 1948; *NEA Journal*

"Japan Loses the War," 1938; *Readers Digest*

"Japanese Children," 1953; *Catholic World*

"Laymen's Mission Report," 1932; *Christian Century*

"The Legend of Tchi-Niu: Adaptation," 1964; *McCalls*

"Let Them Have Reality," 1949; *Child Study*

"Letters to the Editor," 1899; *Christian Observer*

"Letter to Germany," 1946; *Common Ground*

"Letter to the *Times*," 1941; *New York Times*

"Like and Unlike in East and West," 1935; *Vital Speeches*

"Listen to the People, United Nations!," 1947; *United Nations World*

"Literature and Life," 1938; *Saturday Review of Literature*

"Make It Freedom's War," 1942; *New Republic*

"The Man Who Showed China the Vision," 1944; *New York Times Magazine*

"Manners and Civilization," 1942; Johnson, T.H. ed., *Men of Tomorrow*

"A Message to Randolph-Macon," 1943; *Randolph-Macon Woman's College
    Alumnae Bulletin*

"The Mind of the Militarist," 1938; *Asia*

"Missionaries of Empire," 1934; Barnes, J., ed., *Empire in the East*

"The Most Unforgettable Character I've Met," 1946; *Readers Digest*

"Mr. Clinton Stops Starvation," 1949; *United Nations World*
"My Mother's House," 1965; PSB et.al., *My Mother's House*
"My World: American Children: Alien by Birth," 1964; *Ladies Home Journal*
"My World: I Visit Tibet's Dalai Lama," 1965; *Ladies Home Journal*
"My World: To India with Love," 1965; *Ladies Home Journal*
"A New Education for a New Day," 1944; *Virginia Journal of Education*
"New Evidence of the Militarization of America," 1949; PSB et.al.,
       National Council Against Conscription
"New Modes of Chinese Marriage," 1927; *Asia*
"The New Nationalism," 1931; *International Digest*
"The New Patriotism," 1941; *China Weekly Review*
"New Tools for Schools," 1943; *Far Eastern Survey*
"The New Traveler in China," 1946; *Asia and the Americas*
"Nineteen Stockings by the Chimney Piece," 1963; *Readers Digest*
"No Union Without China!," 1941; *Asia*
"A Note on the Price of Rice (and Power)," 1948; *United Nations World*
"An Old Trick of the West," 1939; *Asia*
"On Discovering America," 1937; *Survey Graphic*
"On the Cultivation of a Young Genius," 1937; *Opportunity*
"On the Writing of Novels," 1933; *Randolph-Macon Woman's College
       Alumnae Bulletin*
"An Open Letter to the Chinese People," 1938; *Asia*
"Our Dangerous Myths about China," 1949; *New York Times Magazine*
"Our Last Chance in China," 1944; *Common Sense*
"Pearl Buck," 1939; Fadiman, C., *I Believe*
"Pearl Buck Speaks for Democracy," 1942; *Common Council for American Unity*
"Pearl Buck Talks of Her Life in China," 1932; *China Weekly*
"Pearl S. Buck's Message to New York Chapter," 1935; *Randolph-Macon
       Woman's College Alumnae Bulletin*
"People, East and West," 1943; *Asia and the Americas*
"People in Pain," 1941; *Readers Digest*
"The People Will Be Free," 1948; *United Nations World*
"The Pill and the Teenage Girl," 1967; *Family Week*
"Plain People in China," 1941; *Asia*
"Postwar China and the United States," 1943; *Asia and the Americas*
"President Truman's Point 4," 1950; *Fortnightly*

"Protestant Among the Presbyterians," 1933; *America*
"Protesting an Unfavorable Review of Lillian Smith's 'Killers of the Dream',"
    1949; *New York Times*
"Psychological Setting," 1935; *Institute of Public Affairs*
"Pursuit of Happiness," 1963; *Seventeen*
"A Quarter Century: Its Human Tragedies," 1961; *Look*
"Questions Indians Ask Me," 1946; *Asia and the Americas*
"The Race Barrier That Must Be Destroyed," 1942; *New York Times Magazine*
"Reading and the American Public," 1966; *American Library Assoc. Bulletin*
"The Real Triangle of Life," 1941; *Child Study*
"Recognition and the Writer," 1940; *Saturday Review of Literature*
"Relief—for the American Conscience," 1943; *New York Times Magazine*
"The River," 1931; *Christian Century*
"Room in the Inn," 1950, *Ladies Home Journal*
"Rulers of China," 1935; *Asia*
"Save the Children for What?," 1943; *Journal of Educational Sociology*
"Saving the Good Earth," 1947; *Ave Maria*
"Security in a Cage," 1938; *Survey Graphic*
"Should Gandhi's Assassin Be Killed?," 1948; *United Nations World*
"A Soldier of Japan," 1939; *New Republic*
"Solitary," 1946; *Commentary*
"The Soul of China," 1930; *Living Age*
"The Soul of the East," 1932; *Good Housekeeping*
"The Spirit Behind the Weapon," 1942; *Survey Graphic*
"Spiritual Revulsion," 1942; *Sign*
"Statement on the Founding of the Pearl S. Buck Foundation," 1964; *Insight*
"Take Time to Read Good Books," 1937; *Library Journal*
"Teachers for Fascism's Heirs," 1944; *Common Sense*
"Tell the People," 1945; *Asia and the Americas*
"Thanks to Japan," 1938; *Asia*
"They Who Are Not Yet Born," 1940; *Good Housekeeping*
"Tinder for Tomorrow" ("Asiatic Problems"), 1941; *Post War World Council*
"To My Daughters, With Love," 1967; *Philadelphia Bulletin*
"Total Victory," 1942; *New Republic*
"Tribute to Dr. Machen," 1937; *New Republic*
"Understanding the Chinese," 1944; *Rotarian*

214

"A Visit," 1962; *Suburbia Today*

"A Visit with Pearl Buck," 1971; *National Wildlife*

"Wanted: Real Women" ("Changing Relationships Between Men and Women"), 1962; *Good Housekeeping*

"Warning about China," 1943; *Life*

"Warning to Free Nations," 1941; *Asia*

"We Can Free the Children," 1956; *Woman's Home Companion*

"We Must Quit Playing Santa Claus," 1943; *New York Times Magazine*

"We Need, Most of All, the World View," 1946; *New York Times Magazine*

"We Need the World View," 1948; *Texas Outlook*

"Welcome House," 1958; *Readers Digest*

"Western Weapons in the Hands of the Reckless East," 1937; *Asia*

"What America Means to Me," 1943; *Common Ground*

"What Asians Want," 1951; *Christian Century*

"What Chinese Parents Can Teach Us," 1941; *Parents*

"What I Believe, 1972;" *Encyclopedia British Quarterly*

"What I Learned from Chinese Women," 1972; *Vogue* interview

"What Is Loyalty?," 1953; *Parents Magazine*

"What Religion Means to Me," 1933; *Forum*

"What the Peoples of Asia Want," 1951; *Chicago Council of Foreign Relations*

"What We Are Fighting for in the Orient," 1942; *Christian Science Monitor Magazine*

"When a Daughter Marries," 1949; *Good Housekeeping*

"Where Are the Young Rebels?," 1935; *Harpers*

"Why...Should I Care?," 1932; *Saturday Review of Literature*

"Will a Miracle Child Be Born This Year?," 1970; *Ladies Home Journal*

"Woman of the World," 1947; *United Nations World*

"Woman's Role in the World," 1941; *Independent Woman*

"Women and War," 1940; *Ladies Home Journal*

"The World and the Victor," 1938; *Asia*

"The World of Tomorrow," 1941; *Asia*

"World Understanding through Reading," 1948; *American Library Assoc. Bulletin*

"The Writing of *East Wind: West Wind*," 1932; *Colophan*

"Yen of China," 1948; *United Nations World*

"A Young Chinese Discovers China," 1935; *English Review*

"Your Boy and U. M. T.," 1951; *Christian Century*

COLLECTIONS (FICTION, NONFICTION AND MIXED)

An American Triptych, 1958; 3 Sedges novels
American Unity and Asia, 1942; letters, essays, speeches
The Beech Tree & Johnny Jack and His Beginnings, 1960; juvenile
The Big Wave and Other Stories, 1950; juvenile
China As I See It, 1970; letter, essays, speeches
East and West, 1975; posthumous
Fairy Tales of the Orient, 1965; juvenile
Far and Near: Stories of China, Japan and America, 1947
The First Wife and Other Stories, 1933
Fourteen Stories, 1961
A Gift for the Children, 1973; posthumous
The Good Deed and Other Stories of Asia Past and Present, 1969
Hearts Come Home and Other Stories, 1962
House of Earth, 1935; 3 novels
The Lovers and Other Stories, 1977; posthumous
Mrs. Stoner and the Sea and Other Works, 1976; posthumous; mixed
Once upon a Christmas, 1972; mixed
One Bright Day, and Other Stories for Children, 1952
Pearl S. Buck's Book of Christmas, 1974; posthumous
Secrets of the Heart, 1976; posthumous
The Spirit and the Flesh, 1944; parents' biographies
Stories for Little Children, 1940
Today and Forever, Stories of China, 1941
To My Daughters, With Love, 1967; speeches, essays
Twenty-Seven Stories (Stories of China), 1943
The Water-Buffalo Children and the Dragon Fish, 1966
What America Means to Me, 1943; letters, essays, speeches
The Woman Who Was Changed and Other Stories, 1979; posthumous

JUVENILE

The Beech Tree ("The Heart's Beginning"), 1954
The Big Fight, 1964
The Big Wave, 1947
The Chinese Children Next Door, 1942
The Chinese Story Teller, 1971

216
The Christmas Ghost, 1960
The Christmas Miniature, 1957
The Dragon Fish, 1944
The Good Earth, 1949
Johnny Jack and His Beginnings, 1954
The Little Fox in the Middle, 1966
The Man Who Changed China: The Story of Sun Yat-sen, 1953
"Matthew, Mark, Luke and John," 1966; *Good Housekeeping*
Mrs. Starling's Problem, 1973
My Several Worlds, 1957; abridged
One Bright Day, 1950
The Water-Buffalo Children, 1943
Welcome Child, 1963
The Young Revolutionist, 1932
Yu Lan: Flying Boy of China, 1945

DRAMA
"The Big Wave," 1956; performed on television
"China Speaks to America," 1943; *Asia and the Americas*
"The Chinese Incident," 1942; *Asia*
"Christine," 1960; Broadway musical
"A Desert Incident," 1959; performed in New York
"The Enemy;" performed on television
"The First Wife," 1945; performed on Broadway
"Flight into China" *(Peony)*, 1939; performed in New Jersey
"The No. 1 Christmas Tree in All the World," 1970
"Sun Yat-sen," 1944; *Asia and the Americas*
"Will This Earth Hold?," 1944; *Asia and the Americas*

Index

A Bridge For Passing, 165
A Desert Incident, 162, 163
Actors Will Do Anything (M. Kennedy), 104
Addams, Jane, 133
adoption agencies, Chicago, 99; *see also* Welcome House
adoption; Carie of Precious Cloud, 23; Pearl of Janice Buck, 54-55; John Stulting Walsh, 99; Richard Stulting Walsh, 99; Edgar Walsh, 100; Jean Walsh, 100; speech on, 147-149; *see also* Buck, Pearl S., adoption
African Journey (Robeson), 142
Alice in Wonderland, 29
All Men Are Brothers, translation of *Shui Hu Chuan*, 68; published, 85
All Under Heaven, 182
amah, 46, 62; *see also* Wang Amah
Ambassador, Pearl suggested as, 123-124
Amerasians, difficulties of placing for adoption, 146; plight of in Asian cultures, 146; result of World War II, 146, 147; reunion of girl with her father, 189
America, right of people to be here, 140
America the Beautiful, 33
American Academy of Political and Social Sciences, 52
American Civil Liberties Union, 138

American Library Association, 151
American, gunboats end Nanking Incident, 58; visitors to Asia, Pearl's opinion of, 97; performers in China, 135; on being (Eslanda Goode Robeson), 142
Americans, 23, 134, 139-140
Anand, Dev, 170
Anderson, John, 169, 170
Anderson, Sherwood, 106
Anna and the King of Siam, 92
"arrogant missionary" speech, 76-77
Asia and the Americas, 98; *see also Asia* magazine
Asia magazine, 52, 85, 92, 97, 98, 133
Asian performers, 135
Associated Press, 193
Astor Hotel, Pearl's "arrogant missionary" speech at, 76-77
Atkinson, Brooks, 83, 163
Atlantic City, 151
Atlantic Monthly, 51
Authors Guild, 160
autobiography, Pearl's, 157, 161; *see also My Several Worlds*
Bailey, Dan, 176-178
Baker, Cal, 178
bandits, Pearl's childhood fear of, 25; common in China, 56
Bangkok, 177

218

Beethoven, 132

Bible, *see* Sydenstricker, Absalom, translation of *New Testament*

Bible stories, 20, 83, 100

Big Wave, The, 162, 165, 170

biographies, 88, 107; *see also* Cody, William; *Exile, The*; *Fighting Angel*; *My Several Worlds*

black Americans, 79-80

Black, Dr. Jean, 151

Bleak House, (Dickens), 114

boats, side-wheeler, 6; junk, 7; steamer, 20-21, 24, 30; gunboats, 58; *see also* ships

Bolshevik Revolution, 116

Book-of-the-Month Club, 68, 98, 116, 180

Book Shelf, Pearl's column in Asia magazine, 92; reviews, travel books about Asia, 93; *Of Men and Ideas* (Lin), 93-94; *Glimpses of World History* (Nehru), 96; *Each with his Own Brush* (Fleming), 94-95; reporter's shallow book, 96; *Plant Hunter's Paradise* (Ward), 96; *Far East Policy of the United States* (Griswold), 97

Boxer Rebellion, 23-24

Brandeis, Louis, 133

Brearly School, 89

Breen, George, 154

Breen, Jackie, 154, 157

Britain, 65, 116, 121, 137

British, 23, 39

Broadway, 88, 163

Bromfield, Louis, 133

Bucher, Adeline, 74, 80, 84, 87, 105, 115

Buck family homes, Nanhsuchou, 41, 50; Nanking with Reisners, 43; Nanking, 45, 56, 69; Unzen, Japan, 58, 60; Shanghai, 58, 60,; *see also* Sydenstricker family homes, Walsh family homes

Buck, Caroline Grace (Carol), birth, 43; in Nanking, 45; health, 46, 51-55; in Shanghai, 62; at Training School, 63, 66, 80, 99, 144-145

Buck, Clifford, 84

Buck, Janice, adoption of, 54; cared for by amah, 62; with Miss Bucher, 74; visits Carol, 80; returns to China, 84; voyage to America, 87; attends Brearly School, 89; affection for Carol, 98; relationship with Richard Walsh, 98; assists with children, 100; comes from China, 115; visits stone house, 153

Buck, Lossing, ancestry and birth, 39; agricultural mission, 40; physical characteristics, 40, 75; marriage to Pearl, 41; inspection of mission station, 42; at Nanking University, 43; Master's degree studies, 52; in Unzen, 58, 60; secret journeys to Nanking, 62; frugality of, 63; immersed in work, 69-70; with Lindberghs, 71; receives Ph.D., 84; return to China, 84; trip to Tibet, 86; divorce from Pearl, 90; career (footnote on,) 145; second marriage (footnote on), 145

Buck, Pearl S., *see also* Sydenstricker, Pearl Comfort

acquaintances; Lindberghs, 71; Sinclair Lewis, 106; Dalai Lama, 170; John F. Kennedy, 173; Chou En-Lai, 181; *see also* friends

adoption, The Cradle, 99; speech on, 148; half-Japanese boy, 148; Welcome House, 147-150; *see also* major heading adoption

advisor, college clubs, 35-36; advisory editor John Day Company, 87; consultant on Asian cultures, 92; addresses Chinese performers, 135; president Authors Guild, 160; Pearl

Buck, Pearl S. (continued)
   S. Buck Foundation, 174-176
   appearance, 33, 154, 176; *see also*photos on dustjacket,15, 16, 31, 101, 109, 183
   articles, *Hour of Worship, The*, 37; *In China Too*, 51; *Chinese Woman Speaks, The*, 52, 62; *Revolutionist, The*, 60; *Is There A Case for Foreign Missions?*, 81; *On Discovering America*, 139; *see also* Bibliography, this volume
   awards, best story and poem awards (college), 37; Laura L. Messinger Memorial Prize (graduate school), 52; Pulitzer prize, 74; Nobel Prize for Literature, 105; as John Sedges, 143; honored by Commemorative stamp, 190
   books by, *All Under Heaven*, 182; *American Argument: with Eslanda Goode Robeson*, 142; *Angry Wife, The* (Sedges), 143; *Big Wave, The*, 162, 165, 170; *Child Who Never Grew, The*, 144; *China Flight*, 127; *China Gold*, 127; *Command the Morning*, 162; *Dragon Seed*, 127; *East Wind: West Wind*, 66, 68; *Exile, The*, 63, 88, 98; *Fighting Angel*, 98; *Good Earth, The*, see major heading *Good Earth, The*; *How It Happens: Talk About The German People*, 142; *Imperial Woman*, 159, 182; *Kennedy Women, The*, 173; *Kinfolk*, 144; *Letter from Peking*, 161; *Living Reed, The*, 172; *Long Love, The* (Sedges), 143; *Mandala*, 170-171; *Mother, The*, 82-83; *My Several Worlds*, 157, 161; *Pavilion of Women*, 141; *Peony*, 143; *Promise, The*, 127; *Sons*, 82; *Talk About Russia: With Masha Scott*, 128; *Tell The People: Talks with James Yen about the Mass Education Movement*, 131; *This Proud Heart*, 108; *Three Daughters of Madame Liang, The*, 180; *Townsman, The*, (Sedges), 128, 143; *Rainbow, The*, 182; *Voices in the House*, (Sedges), 156; number of books written, 193; *see also* Bibliography, this volume
   character, desire for privacy, 187-188; as a fighter against wrong, 190; described by M. Roebling, 190-192; *see also* appearance, interests, philanthropy
   childhood, birth and ancestry, 3-4, 6; as toddler, 8-9; relationship with father, 17-18, 25, 34; childhood lessons about America, 32, 80; love of books, 19; travel on steamer, 20; studies of Bible stories, 24; duties during Chinese famine, 25-26; childhood fear of bandits, 25; sense of orderliness, 27; characteristics like Carie, 28
   children, Carol Buck, 43; Janice Buck, 54; John Stulting Walsh, 99; Richard Stulting Walsh, 99; Edgar Walsh, 100; Jean Walsh, 100; Henriette Walsh, 156; Chieko Walsh, 159; Johanna Walsh, 159; Teresa Walsh, 159; Julie Henning Walsh, 179
   college (at Randolph-Macon Woman's College), 29-30, 33-37
   commendations for, 130, 155-156, 181; *see also* criticism
   correspondence, 104, 120-121, 122
   criticism of, 77, 81, 91, 106, 130, 139, 155, 163, 190-192
   death of, 182-185
   education, 19, 24, 26, 32, 52, 82; *see*

220

Buck, Pearl S. (continued)
  also Buck, Pearl S., college
    employment, 37, 39, 52, 133
  family, pregnancy, 43; birth of Carol,
    43; with baby Janice at in-laws'
    farm, 55; relationships with
    stepchildren, 99; devotion to
    Richard, 124; balancing career and
    marriage, 143; attitude during
    Richard's illness, 157; having a
    retarded daughter, 164; Richard's
    death, 164, 165; *see also* Buck, Pearl
    S., adoption, children, marriage
  friends; meeting Eleanor Roosevelt,
    53; Mrs. Lu's "Wise Mother," 55;
    respect for Richard Walsh, 65; Lin
    Yutang, 115; Tsuta Lombard, 134;
    Tad Danielewski, 170; Ernest
    Hocking, 172
  homes, penthouse overlooking East
    River, 87; Murray Hill (Malvina
    Hoffman home), 89; Forest Haunt,
    154, 155; *see also* Buck family
    homes, Sydenstricker family homes,
    Walsh family homes
  languages, 19, 32, 74, 82
  letters, *see* correspondence
  love, *see* romance
  marriage, thoughts on, 39; to Lossing,
    41; to Richard, 90
  mission, 82; *see also* romance
  nicknames, Wise Mother, 50, 56, 57,
    58; Miss Chinahand Buck, 106;
    Gran, 149; Miss Pearlbuck, 159;
    The Empress, 174, 182
  philanthropy, 25-26, 68, 80, 83-85,
    88, 134, 147, 151, 176, 184
  plays, pens unnamed play, 88;
    Empress, The, 102-104; *Crystal
    Heart, The,* 102; *Flight into China,*
    102; *My Indian Family,* 163; *see
    also* Bibliography this volume

  politics, 111, 123, 138, 139
  positions, *see* advisor
  religion, family religion, 3; similarities
    of Buddhism, Christianity, 29;
    "heretic" at boarding school, 29;
    religious belief, 95; love of science
    and religion, 124
  romance, 38, 40, 84, 124, 125, 192;
    see also marriage
  self-image, 28, 33, 172; *see also* character
  speeches, American Academy of
    Political Sciences, 53; "arrogant
    missionaries" speech at Astor Hotel,
    76-77; before professional black
    women in Harlem, 79; New School
    for Social Research, 80; commence-
    ment speech at Randolph-Macon,
    82; Virginia University Inst. of
    Public Affairs, 91-92; Nobel Prize
    Acceptance Speech, 108-110; in
    Denmark on China's future (refer-
    ence only), 111; California Senate
    Committee on Japanese Americans,
    138; on patriotism, 139; adopting
    Amerasians, 148
  travels, voyage to China, 6; on steamer,
    20; during World War I, 38; on
    sedan chair, 42; return to China,
    84; in China with Richard, 86-87;
    to America, 87; to India with Tad
    Danielewski, 169; plans to visit
    China in late life, 181; *see also* fur-
    lough
  views on, Lewis Carroll, 29; America,
    32; orderliness, 35; change, 92;
    goodwill, 93; practical values, 93;
    modern Chinese mind, 93-94; trav-
    el books about Asia, 93; tyranny,
    93; Chinese courage, 94; cultures,
    94; Buddhism, 95; Hinduism, 95;
    history, 95-96; life, 95; mysticism,
    95; ecology, 96; foreign students'

goals, 96; passionate pursuit of ideas, 96; Americans in Asia, 97; U.S. Far East Policy, 97; Sinclair Lewis's genius, 106; future, value of, (Nobel Prize Speech), 108; winning Nobel Prize, 110; Chinese feelings about Americans, 121; plight of bomb victims in Hiroshima, 122; race relations, 123; Russian people, 128-130; peace, 131; Chinese performers, 135; Chinese people, 137; McCarthyism, 137; giving people a chance, 139; safety through diversity in America, 139; balancing career and marriage, 143; plight of Amerasians in Asian cultures, 146; prejudice suffered, 146; hybrid peoples, 147; establishing Welcome House, 146-148; wisecracks as communication, 157; having a retarded daughter, 164; coincidence, 166; doing good works, 166; faith, 166; life after death, 166; the Dalai Lama, 170; most needy children, 174; America's responsibility to Amerasian children, 174; privacy, 187; temporariness, 187-188

writings, first in China, 19, 27; decision to become writer, 51; first sale to *Asia* magazine, 52; book contract with John Day Company, 70; reactions to reviews of *The Good Earth*, 69; collaboration with Lin Yutang, 116; writing as John Sedges, 127; essay *On Discovering America*, 139; *see also* Buck, Pearl S., articles, books, plays, Bibliography this volume

Bucks County, 123, 165

Buffalo Bill, *see* Cody, William

Buffalo, New York, 64

Burbank, Luther, 134

Burgess, Perry, 133

Burma, 4

Burpee, David, 149

Burpee, Lois, 149

Camellia House, greenhouse at Green Hills Farm, 115

Canton, 19

capitalism, 130; *see also* imperialism, Communism, Collective

capitalists, 139

Carie, *see* Sydenstricker, Carie

Carlisle, Kitty, 150

Carol Cottage, at Training School, 80

Carroll, Lewis, 29

Carter, Elmer, 79

Carver, George Washington, 133

caseworkers in Asia, 176-178

CBS (Columbia Broadcasting System), 161, 162

Central American performers, 134

Chang, Lomay, (footnote on), 145

Chaplin, Charlie, 138

Chengtu, 131

Chew, Joseph, 113

Chiang Kai-shek, 56, 60, 111, 116, 120, 121, 137

Chicago, 99

Child Who Never Grew, The, 145

children, rights of (UN Charter), 198

China and the West, speech, 52;

China Flight, 127

China Gold, 127

China, return to by Buck family, 84; trip to by Richard Walsh, 86; freedom in (Nobel Prize Speech) 110; race relations, 123; People's Republic of, 137; Pearl's plans to visit, 181

Chinese

Ambassador Hu Shih, 40

Christians, 12, 24

Chinese (continued)
  concessions, 24, 32
  consulate, 181
  coolies, 42
  crime, killing of infant girls, 7; robbers
    of Absalom, 13; pickpockets, 21;
    prostitution, 29; slavery implied, 29;
    banditry, 56; kidnapping, 61
  customs, polygamy, 20, 61-62; bind-
    ing of girls' feet, 23; marriage of
    eldest daughter, 39
  dialects, book of by Absalom, 56
  Emperors, Hsien Feng, 10; T'ung
    Chih, 10; Kuang Hsu, 11
  government, under Sun Yat-sen, 39,
    42; under Chiang Kai-shek, 56-57,
    120-121; under Communism, 137,
    181; Nationalist Party, 56, see also
    Kuomingtang
  history, Manchu Dynasty, 10-11;
    Boxer Rebellion, 23-24, famine,
    25-26; Republic under Sun Yat-
    Sen, 39, 42-43; under Chiang Kai-
    shek, 56-57, 120-121; Yangtse
    flood, 71; Japanese invasion, 73;
    novelists ignored in, 76; in Book
    Shelf review, 95; civil war, 116;
    World War II, 120-121; Mass
    Education Movement under James
    Yen, 131-132; People's Republic of
    China, 137
  illiteracy of in France, 131
  language, Carie, 8; nursery rhymes of
    Wang Amah, 9; Pearl, 19, 68, 82,
    85; Lossing Buck, 40; written lan-
    guage simplified by James Yen, 120
  New Testament, Absalom's transla-
    tion of, 11, 20, 30, 48; printed and
    bound, 74
  orderliness, 27, 35, 180; influences
    The Townsman, 128
  people, 12, 28, 70, 131, 135, 137

  philosophy, on male children, 8, 65;
    on foreigners, 12; on Christianity,
    77; contrast with puritanism, 92; of
    problem-solving, 166
  preachers, 49
  proverbs, 48, 71, 159
  Red Cross, 58
  warlords, battle Kuomingtang, 56
  wheat industry, 40
  winters, 22
Chinkiang, 19, 38, 48
Chopin, 132
Chou En-Lai, 181
Christ, 22, 76, 81
Christine, 163
Christmas, 21, 25, 34, 43, 145
Chungking, 121
churches, local in West Virginia, 25;
    Madison Avenue Presbyterian, 40;
    First Presbyterian Troy, NY, 54; see
    also mission house
City of Tokio, 6
Cliveden, 113
clothing; Absalom's love of Chinese, 9;
    dressing for steamer travel, 20; famine
    hats, 28; Pearl's Chinese grass linen
    dress, 33; Pearl's Chinese brocaded
    jackets, 115; Pearl's honorary doctor-
    ate robes, 115
Clume-Seymour, Sir Michael and Lady
    Faith, 115
Cody, William "Buffalo Bill," 66, 123
Coffin, Dr. Henry Sloan, 40
Collective, 129; see also Communism
colleges/universities, Bryn Mawr, 36;
    Columbia University, 134, 189;
    Cornell Agricultural College, 40;
    Cornell University, 52, 74, 84;
    Harvard, 65-66; Nanking University
    43; Oberlin College, 131; Portland
    State University, 151; Princeton
    University, 116; Randolph-Macon

Woman's College, 33-37, 82; University of Peking Medical College, 87; Vanport Community College, 151; Virginia University, 91; Wellesley, 29; Yale University, 82

Collier's magazine, 66

Coltman, Bob, 115

Coltman, Natalie Walsh, 115

Command the Morning, 162

Commemorative stamp, 190

Communism, compared to capitalism, imperialism, 130; Pearl accused of, 139

Communist, battle Kuomingtang, 56; agents provoke Nanking Incident, 57; compared to Collective, 129; propaganda, *Talk With Russia* labeled as, 130; infiltration, charges of in East and West Assoc., 137; *see also* Communism, McCarthyism, FBI

concubines, 20, 61, 69

Confucius, 29

Connecticut, 154

Cornell Agricultural College, *see* Cornell University

Cornell University, Lossing Buck's alma mater, 40; Bucks' Masters programs, 52; Pearl's meeting with Eleanor Roosevelt, 53; Lossing Buck's Ph.D. work, 74, 84

Cornell, Katherine, American actress, 102, 103;

correspondence school, 49, 56

Cosmopolitan Club, 103

Cosmopolitan, 81, 88

Covarrubias, Miguel, 133

Cowles, Fleur, 122

Cradle, The, 99

Crawford, Joan, 174

criticism, critics, *see* Buck, Pearl S., commendation and criticism

Crucifixion, The, 159

Crystal Heart, The, 103

culture, 8, 92

Dalai, Lama, 170

Danielewski, Tad, 161-163, 169-170

Daniels, Dr. Horton, 45

Davis, Owen, Jr., 74

Davis, Owen, 74

death, of Carie's first children, 3-4; of Chinese Emperors, 10-11; of Clyde Sydenstricker, 21; of Hermanus Stulting, 32; of Wang Amah 36; of Dowager Empress, 39; of Carie, 47; of Absalom, 71; of Anne Yaukey, 100; of Edgar Sydenstricker, 100; of Richard, 164; of Pearl, 182-184

Decator, Priscilla, 170

Delaware, 174

Denmark, 111

Desert Incident, A, 163, 164

desk, *Good Earth*, 113-114

Dewey, John, 133

Dickens, Charles, 114

divorce, 36, 90

Door of Hope, 29

Douglas, Helen, 122

Dowager Empress (Tz'u Hsi), hatred of missionaries, 11; edict to kill foreigners, 23; flight to Sian, 24; murder of Pearl Concubine, 24; concessions to foreign powers, 24; death of, 39; as inspiration for *Imperial Woman*, 159

Dragon Seed, 127, 137

Dreiser, Theodore, 105, 106

Droop Mountain, 25

Dublin, Bucks County, Pennsylvania, 113, 188

Dutch, 39

Each with his Own Brush (Fleming), 94

East and West Association, 88, 133-135, 137

East Wind: West Wind, 66, 68

Edison, Thomas Alva, 134

editor, *New York Times*, 63; Richard

224

Walsh as, 85; Pearl as, 87, 92
Edmunds, Emma, 33, 68, 82
Eisenhower, Dwight D., 122, 174, 189
Eldridge, Florence, 138
Empress Consort, Tz'u An, 10
Empress Dowager Tz'u Hsi, 10; *see also*
   Dowager Empress
Empress of Britain, 84
Empress of Russia, 87
Empress, The, 102-104
Empress, The, nickname for Pearl, 174,
   182; *see also* Buck, Pearl S., nicknames
Enemy, The, 162
England, 32; *see also* Britain
ESP (extra-sensory perception), 171
European powers, 23
Exile, The, 63, 88, 98
Fadiman, Clifton, 123
Fall River, Massachusetts, 100
famine, Great Chinese, 25, 28
Faulkner, William, 106, 139, 155
FBI, 139
Fermi, Enrico, 107-108
Field, Marshall, 122
Fighting Angel, 98
Finley, Dr. John F., Jr., 63
Finley, Mrs. John F., 63
First Presbyterian Church, 54
Fischer, Kermit, 149
Fischer, Margaret, 149
Fisher, Dorothy Canfield, 122
Fleming, Daniel, 94
Flight into China, 102, 116, 143
Fontanne, Lynn, 102
Ford Hook Farm, 150
Ford, Henry Jr., 122, 133
Foreigner's Cemetery, 4, 21, 48
Forest Haunt, 154, 155
France, 32, 131; *see also* French
Franklin Delano Roosevelt Library, 120
French, 23, 32, 39, 60, 171
French-Huguenot, 4

freshman English rumor, 35
Friday Literary Club, 29
Frost, Robert, 106
furlough, from mission field,
   Sydenstrickers, 3, 24, 30; Bucks, 63, 74
Galla, Mrs., 182, 184
Gandhi, Indira, 122
Geary Theater, 188
Geneva, 73
George Washington Carver, 133
Gerhart, Sumi Mishima, 149
Germantown, Pennsylvania, 113
Germany, 4, 23
Gilbert and Sullivan, 158
Gillmore, Margalo, 103
Glimpses of World History (Nehru), 96
God, 7, 10, 18, 24, 70, 166-167
Good Earth desk, 113
Good Housekeeping, 181
Good Earth, The, movie, 100-101; novel,
   68-70, 73-74, 82, 106, 128, 192;
   stage play, 74, 82-83
Grace, Princess of Monaco, 174
Grand Canal, 7
"Great Battle," of New Testament trans-
   lation, 30
Great Depression, 85, 130
Great Flood, of Yangtse River, 71
Green Hills Farm, 88-89, 91, 113-115,
   149, 156, 159, 164, 182, 184, 188,
   190
Greenbrier County, 5
Gregg, Richard, 153
Griswold, A. W., 97
Guide, The, 169, 170
Guild Theatre, 83
Gustaf, King of Sweden, 108-109
Hamburg, Germany, 142
Hammerstein, Dorothy, 150
Hammerstein, Oscar II, Broadway pro-
   ducer, 150
Hankow, 30, 121

Harlem, 79, 123
Harper's magazine, 81
Harvard University, 65-66
Hayes, Helen, 103
Henning, Julie Walsh, adopted child of Pearl, 179-180
Hepburn, Katherine, 137, 138
heresy, charges against Pearl, 81
Hidden Flower, The, 155
Hillsboro, West Virginia, 3
Hiroshima, 122
Hocking, Ernest, 172
Hoelsing, Admiral W. F., 133
Hoffman, Malvina, 89
Holland, 4
Holmes, Oliver Wendell, 133
Honan, China, 143
Horne, Lena, 138
Horton, Mildred McAfee, 133
Hotels, Waldorf Astoria, 75, 122; Astor, site of Pearl's "arrogant missionary" speech, 76-77
Hour of Worship, The, 37
How It Happens: Talk About The German People, 142
Hsien Feng, Chinese Emperor, 10
Hsu Chih-mo, Chinese poet, (footnote on), 141
Hu Shih, friend of Lossing, 40; ambassador to America, 93
Hughes, Langston, 138
Huston, John, 138
Hwang, Squire, in *The Good Earth*, 69
hybrid peoples, 147
Hyde Park, New York, 121
immigration laws, 120
Imperial Woman, 159
imperialism, 130, *see also* capitalism, Collective
In China Too, 51
India League of America, 122, 135
India, 123, 169-171

Indo-China, 86
Israel, 193
Is There A Case For Foreign Missions? 81
Ithaca, New York, 52, 53, 74, 83
Jade Room, in Waldorf Astoria, 75
Jagat, Prince, in *Mandala*, 171
Janeway, Elizabeth, 155-156
Japan, 6, 58, 73; *see also* Unzen
Japanese, 23, 57, 58, 73, 120, 180
Jewell, Eugenia and Martha, 28, 29
Jews of Kaifengfu, The (footnote on), 143
John Day Company, 64, 66, 70, 85, 87, 144, 162
Johnstone, Dr. Edward, 63, 80
Judson, Ann Hasseltine, 4
Junior East and West Clubs, 135
junk, 7, *see also* boats, ships
Kaifengfu, 143
Kalpana, 188-189
Kansas City, 192
Kansas, 128
Kappa Delta sorority, 36
Kaye, Danny, 138
Kaye, Miss, 100, 107
Keller, Helen, 134
Kennedy, John F., 173
Kennedy, Mary, 103, 104
Kennedy, Rose, 181
Kennedy Women, The, 173
kidnapping, 80-81
Kinfolk, 144
King, Gustaf of Sweden, 108-109
Korea, 59, 165, 172, 173, 174
Korean War, 137, 193
Krebs, Albin, 184
Kuling, 40, 71
Kung family, 173
Kung, Prince, brother of Hsien Feng, 10; as diplomat, 11
Kuomingtang, 56; *see also* Chinese government
Ladies' Home Journal, 144, 156, 170

Lagerlof, Selma, 106, 110

Lake Tahoe, 90

Larrimore, 82, 83

Latin American performers, 134

League of Nations, 73

Letter from Peking, 161

letters, *see* Buck, Pearl S., correspondence

Lewis, Ardron, 84

Lewis, Sinclair, 106

Li Lien-ying, 11

Liang, Dr., in *Kinfolk,* 144

libraries, at Green Hills Farm, 113, 114; Franklin Delano Roosevelt Library, 120; Vanport Community College affected by flood, 151; Books for the Blind, 158; at Ernest Hocking's home, 172

Lin Mousheng, 93

Lin Yutang, 86, 115, 116, 144

Lindbergh, Colonel Charles and Mrs., 71, 81

Lindsay, Vachel, 185

literacy, Russian peasants, 130; Chinese peasants, 131-132

literary agents, 62, 87, 159; *see also* Lloyd, David, Olding, Dorothy

Literary Guild, 141

Little Meatball, 50, 55

Little Meatball II, 62

Liverpool, 84

Living Reed, The, 172

Lloyd, David, literary agent, 62, 64, 68, 70, 73, 159

Lombard, Mary Tsuta Ohata, 134

Loris, Mrs., cook, 107

Lu, Mrs., 50, 55, 57, 58, 60-62

Luce, Henry, 122, 133

Lunt, Alfred, 102

Lynchburg, Virginia, 29, 30, 33

Machen, Reverend J. Gresham, 81

MacMahon, Aline, 137

Magnitogorsk, 130

Main Street, (Lewis), 106

Manchu Dynasty, 10, *see also* Empress Dowager

Mandala, 170, 171

Manila, 38

March, Frederic, 138

dangerous persons, suspected of Communism, 138

marriage, Pearl and Lossing Buck, 41; Grace and Jesse Yaukey, 51; Mrs. Lu, 61; Pearl and Richard Walsh, 90; devotion in Pearl's and Richard's, 124

Martha's Vineyard, 116

Mass Education Movement, 131, 132

Mayo Clinic, 54

McCarthy, Joseph, *see* McCarthyism

McCarthyism, 127, 137

McClintic, Guthrie, 102

McNutt, Paul, 133

Mead, Margaret, 122, 133

Mencken, H. L., 155

MGM, film rights to *The Good Earth,* 73

Mission Board, 63, 66, 70, 76

mission field, 48, 82

mission house, 7, 18, 23

missionaries, attitude on Chinese, 11; missionary-baiting, 21; force Absalom's resignation, 48; cable State Department about Kuomingtang, 56; Presbyterian, 75; labeled arrogant by Pearl, 76-77; anger at Pearl, 77, 99; condemn Chinese, 81; criticism of Pearl's marriage to Richard, 91

mixed-blood children, 20, 145 *see also* Amerasians

Modern Literary Club, 36

Moment in Peking (Lin), 115

Montreal, 74

Moon Over Burma (footnote on), 136

Moran, Judge Thomas F., 90

Morrison, Robert, 10

Mother, The, 82-83; *see also* trilogy

Muni, Paul, 100
Murray Hill, 89
My Indian Family, 163
My Several Worlds, 157, 161
Nanhsuchou, 41, 50
Nanking, 43, 45, 49, 56-57, 59, 63
Nanking Incident, 56-57, 60
Nanking University, 43
Nationalist, *see* Kuomingtang
Nazimova, Alla, 82, 83
Nazism, 142
NBC (National Broadcasting Company), 135, 162, 163
Nearing, Scott, 153
Nehru, Jawaharlal, 93, 96, 121, 189
New Haven, Connecticut, 163
New Jersey, 88
New Rochelle, New York, 165
New School for Social Research, 80
New Testament in Chinese, 11, 20, 30, 48, 74
New York City, 40, 62, 64, 70, 75, 83, 100, 114, 116, 123, 135, 137
New York Daily Mirror, 163
New York Herald Tribune, 69, 75
New York Post, 81, 144
New York Times Book Review, 98
New York Times, 63, 163
New Yorker magazine, 104
Newspapers, Shanghai, 27; Lynchburg, 30; *New York Times*, 63, 163; *New York Herald Tribune*, 69, 75; *New York Post*, 81, 144; *New York Times Book Review*, 98; *New York Daily Mirror*, 163; *San Francisco Chronicle*, 184
Nice, France, 84
Nixon, Richard M., 181, 184
Nobel Prize, for Literature won by Pearl, 105-106; for Physics won by Enrico Fermi, 107; acceptance speech, 108-110; displayed at Green Hills Farm, 115; Nobel Prize Winners dinner, 173
notable Americans, Addams, Jane, 133; Brandeis, Louis, 133; Burbank, Luther 134; Carver, George Washington, 133; Dewey, John, 133; Edison, Thomas Alva, 134; Ford, Henry, Jr., 133; Holmes, Oliver Wendell, 134; Keller, Helen, 134, Rogers, Will, 134; Roosevelt, Franklin D., 134; Roosevelt, Theodore, 134; Twain, Mark, 133; Washington, Booker T., 134; Wilson, Woodrow, 133
Nurse Kaye, *see* Kaye, Miss
nurse, Carie's English, 46-47
O'Hara, Maureen, 163
O-lan, on stage by Alla Nazimova, 82; in movie by Luise Rainer, 102
obituary, Pearl's, 184
Occident, 144
Of Men and Ideas (Lin), 93-94
Olding, Dorothy, 159
Oliver Twist (Dickens), 114
Onward Christian Soldiers, 18
On Discovering America, 139
opium, 12, 17, 20
Opportunity magazine, 79
Orient, 144
orphanage, 54, 164
Osterling, Anders, 107
Ottinger, Walsh chauffeur, 157
P.E.N., writer's association, 106
Pacific Northwest, 151
Pahk Induk, 93
Pandit, Madame, 122
Pavilion of Women, 141
Pearl Concubine, 24
Pearl S. Buck Foundation, 174-178
People's Philosopher, The, *see* Hocking, Ernest
Peking, 19, 77
Penn Ridge High School, 179

Pennsylvania Dutch couple, see Yoder, Lloyd and Viola

Pennsylvania Dutch grocer, 147

Peony, 143

People's Republic of China, 137, 181; see also China, Chinese

People's schools, in Mass Education Movement, 132

Peoples East and West, course on, 135

Phelps, William Lyons, 82

phenylketonuria (PKU), 145

Philadelphia, 53, 81, 82, 83, 179

Pleasant Valley Farm, 75, 90

Polo, Marco, 123

Poughkeepsie, 39, 45

Precious Cloud, see Sydenstricker, Precious Cloud

prejudice, 59, 79, 116, 134, 146, 148

Presbyterian, 40, 41, 45, 82

Price, Vincent, 103

prisoner, Mrs. Lu_s in Buck home, 61

professors, comments about Pearl, 35

Promise, The, 127

Provisional Committee to a Democratic Peace, 123

pseudonym, Pearl as John Sedges, 127

Pulitzer Prize, 70, 74-76

Purple Mountain, 66

Pusan, 179

Quaker Hostel, 123

Radio City Music Hall, 137

Rainbow, The, 182

Rainer, Luise, 102

Randolph-Macon Woman's College, 29, 33-37

Reader's Digest, 180

Red Russians, 129

reincarnation, 170, 171

Reischauer, Edwin, 133

Reisner, Bertha, 43

Reisner, Dean John, 43

religion, Pearl's family, 3; persecution of

Stulting family, 4; Chinese view of Christian, 76-77

Reno, 90

reviews, *The Good Earth* by Will Rogers, 74; *The Good Earth* stage play, 83; see also *Book Shelf* reviews

Revolutionist, The, 60

Reynal and Hitchcock, publishers, 87

Righteous Uniting Band, 23; see also Boxer Rebellion

rights, of people to be in America, 140; of children (UN Charter), 198

Rimington, Critchell, 86, 87

Robert Montgomery Show, 162

Robeson, Eslanda Goode, 142

Robeson, Paul, 142

Rockefeller, Nelson, 122

Rockingham Castle, 114

Rodgers, Richard, 150

Roebling, Mary G., 190, 193

Rogers, Will, 74, 134

Romulo, Carlos, 93

Roosevelt, Eleanor, 53, 120-122

Roosevelt, Franklin D., 121, 134

Roosevelt, Theodore, 134

Ross, Ishbel, 75

Russia, 30, 128-130

Russian, 30, 116, 129

"Saints and Sinners," 19

San Francisco Chronicle, 184

San Francisco, 6

Sauk Centre, Minnesota, 106

Sawada, Miki, 159, 164, 165

Scott, John, 128, 129, (footnote on) 130, 153

Scott, Masha, 128, 129, 130

Sedges, John, see Buck, Pearl S., books by

Selznick, Myron, 104

Senior Club, 36

Shanghai lace, 41

Shanghai, 4, 6, 24, 27, 28, 38, 40, 46, 58, 60

Shankar, Uday, 188
Sheridan, Wyoming, 157
ships, *City of Tokio*, 6; American war-
  ship, 58; *Empress of Britain*, 84;
  Empress of Russia, 87
Shui Hu Chuan, 68; published as *All
  Men Are Brothers*, 85
Sian, 24
Silver and Prices in China (L. Buck), 89
Simonson, Lee, 75
Sino-Japanese War, 97
Skinner, Cornelia Otis, 103
slums, American, 79; Asian, 176-178
Smith, Margaret, 122
Snell, Dr. George, 147
Snow, Edgar, 86
Snow, Helen Foster, 86
Solomon, Charles M., 173, 178
Sons, 82, *see also* trilogy
South Carolina, 142
Southern Presbyterian Board of Foreign
  Missions, 12, 37; *see also* Mission
  Board
Southern Presbyterian, 3, 5, 10, 29
speeches, *see* Buck, Pearl S., speeches
St. Paul, 18
Stamm, Dr. Frederick, 150, 164
Stamm, Mrs. Frederick, 150
Standard Oil Company, 38
steamer, travel on Yangtse, 20, 30;
  escape during Boxer Rebellion, 24
Steward, Mrs. Celia, 52
Stevenson, Adlai, 122
Stratton Mountain, 154
Stratton Productions, 163, 165, 170
Student Committee, 35
Student Volunteer Movement, 36
students, visitors to Buck home, 45;
  treatment of foriegn, 53
Stulting family, origin of, 4
Stulting Place, the, 3
Stulting, Cornelius, 18, 22, 25, 32

Stulting, Hermanus, 25, 32
Sun Yat-sen, 39, 42, 56
Sweden, site of Nobel Prize ceremony,
  107
Swedish Academy, 107, 111
Swedish-American Society, 111, 113
Sydenstricker, Absalom
  biography Fighting Angel, 98; see also
    Buck, Pearl S., relationship with
    father
  church and missionary work, 7, 10,
    11, 18, 24, 25, 33-34, 48-49, 59,
    62
  death and burial of, 71; voice from
    grave, 167
  family, 3, 5, 49, 71
  illness, 56
  travels, itinerant 5, 10, 17; donkey,
    12, 13; mule and wagon, 12-13,
    17; see also furlough
  views on, marriage, 5; children, 6;
    religion, 5, 10,; Chinese clothes, 9,
    20; fellow missionaries, 11; magis-
    trates, 11; Chinese people, 12; birth
    of Christ, 21; Americans in China,
    32; education, 40; Koreans, 59;
    reaction to The Good Earth, 70
  writings, translation of New
    Testament, 11, 20, 30, 48, 74;
    book of Chinese dialects, 56
Sydenstricker, Alice, 33, 34, 35, 36
Sydenstricker, Carie (Caroline Stulting),
  biography, 98; *see also Exile, The*
  character, 4, 7, 22-23, 32, 47
  death and burial of, 47, 48
  family, 3, 6, 7, 36
  prophecies, Pearl's marriage to
    Lossing to fail, 41
  skills, 8, 18, 22, 23, 25, 27, 32, 40, 80
  views on, children, 3, 5, 7; junks, 7;
    religion, 8, 37; Christmas, 21; edu-
    cation, 40 (see also skills)

Sydenstricker, child of Edgar (unnamed), 33

Sydenstricker, Christopher, 5

Sydenstricker, Clyde, 9, 17-18, 21

Sydenstricker, Deborah, 5

Sydenstricker, Edgar, 6; as elder son, 8 (*see also* cultural differences); on steamer, 20; education in America, 22; home and career in Lynchburg, Virginia, 30; squabbles with Alice, 34; disintegration of marriage, 34, 35, 36; posted to Washington, D.C., 37; visits Pearl at Pleasant Valley Farm, 55; betrays Pearl's travels, 74; economist and researcher, 89; home near Green Hills Farm, 89; death of, 100

Sydenstricker family, 4, 5, 20-22, 30, 32

Sydenstricker family homes, Tsingkiangpu, 7; mission house, 18, 23; Chinkiang, 19, 49; Kuling, 19, 40; Shanghai, 24; Nanking, 49

Sydenstricker, Grace, birth, 22; babyhood, 23; bridesmaid, 41; college, 45-46; care of mother, 47; marriage, 51; *see also* Yaukey, Grace

Sydenstricker, Pearl Comfort, 3, 36, 40; *see also* Buck, Pearl S.

Sydenstricker, Precious Cloud, 22, 24

Szechuan, 131

Taiwan, 137

"talk book," by Pearl, 128, 142; *American Argument: with Eslanda Goode Robeson*, 142; *How It Happens: Talk About The German People*, 142; *Talk about Russia: With Masha Scott*, 128; *Tell The People: Talks with James Yen about the Mass Education Movement*, 131; *see also* Buck, Pearl S., books by

Talk About Russia: With Masha Scott, 128

Talks with Masha, serialized version of

Talk About Russia, 128

Tao, Uncle, character in *Kinfolk*, 144

Tattler, The, college magazine at Randolph-Macon Woman's college, 36, 37

Tell The People...Mass Education Movement, 131

Tenney, Senator Jack, 138

Theatre Guild, 74, 75, 88

This Proud Heart, 108

Thomas, Lowell, 76

Thompson, Dorothy, 122

Thompson, Rev. R. C., 90

Thoughts on Death and Life (Hocking), 172

Three Daughters of Madame Liang, The, 180

Tibet, 86

Tientsin, 24

Time magazine, 172

Toho Film Production Company, 163

Townsman, The, first John Sedges novel, 128, 143

Training School, 63, 80, 88

Treasure Room, at Green Hills Farm, 115

Treasury Department, 89

trilogy, (includes *The Good Earth, Sons, The Mother*), 82

Trippe, Juan, 133

Troy, New York, 54

Truehart, Charles, 139

Truman, Harry S., 122

Tsingkiangpu, 7

Tsuta, *see* Lombard, Mary

Twain, Mark, 133

Tz'u An, *see* Empress Consort Tz'u An

Tz'u Hsi, *see* Dowager Empress, Empress Dowager Tz'u Hsi

United Nations, 135; *see also* League of Nations

United Nations World magazine, 98; *see*

also Asia, Asia and the Americas
United States government, 32, 146
Unzen, Nagasaki Prefecture, Japan, 58;
    Pearl writes in, 60
Vancouver, B.C., port of entry, 74, 87
Venice, 84
Vermont, 28, 75, 153, 165
Vietnam, 137
Vietnam War, 193
Vineland School, *see* Training School
Virginia University, 91
Voices in the House (Sedges), 156
Von Kettler, Baron, 23
Von Pustau, Erna, 142
Waldorf Astoria Hotel, 75, 122
Walsh family homes, Green Hills Farm
    (*see* major heading Green Hills Farm);
    Park Avenue, 99; stone house, 153;
    Forest Haunt, 154
Waechter, Elisabeth, 150
Walsh, Betty, daughter of Richard and
    Ruby Walsh, 107
Walsh, Chieko, adopted by Pearl and
    Richard, 159, 165
Walsh, Edgar, adopted by Pearl and
    Richard, 100
Walsh, Henriette, adopted by Pearl and
    Richard, 156, 165
Walsh, Jean, adopted by Pearl and
    Richard, 100
Walsh, Johanna, adopted by Pearl and
    Richard, 159, 165
Walsh, John Stulting, adopted by Pearl
    and Richard, 99
Walsh, Julie Henning, adopted by Pearl,
    179
Walsh, Mrs. Pearl S., *see* Buck, Pearl S.,
Walsh, Natalie, *see* Coltman, Natalie
Walsh, Richard "Dick," Jr., son of
    Richard and Ruby (not to be confused
    with Richard Stulting Walsh), 134
Walsh, Richard Stulting, adopted by

Pearl and Richard, 99
Walsh, Richard
    appearance, photo, 67; 154
    associates, Lin Yutang, 86
    business manager, 81, 82, 83, 122-
    123
    character, 65, 70, 77, 124, 157, 164
    death and burial, 157-158, 164, 165
    employment, other, 66; see also
        Walsh, Richard, publisher
    families, three children by Ruby, 66;
        divorce from Ruby, 90; marriage to
        Pearl, 90; affection for Carol Buck,
        98, 99
    illness, terminal, 157-158
    publisher, accepts "Winds of
        Heaven," 64; purchases John Day
        Company, 66; renames "Wang
        Lung" manuscript The Good
        Earth, 68; book contract with
        Pearl, 70; financial troubles, 66, 85;
        saves John Day Company, 87; buys
        Asia magazine, 92; publishes Asian
        writers, 93
    romance, 89
    travels, 84, 86-87, 157
    writings, 66, 85-86
Walsh, Ruby, 66, 81, 84, 90
Walsh, Teresa, adopted by Pearl and
    Richard, 159
Wang Amah, nanny, 6, 7, 8, 9, 18, 22,
    26, 36
Wang Lung, in *The Good Earth* novel,
    68, 69; stage play, 82; movie, 100
war, Opium Wars, 12; Boxer Rebellion,
    23; Korea, 137, 193; Sino-Japanese,
    97; Vietnam, 137, 193; World War I,
    38, 130, 131; World War II, 97, 120,
    121, 136, 146, 190, 193
Ward, F. Kingdon, 96
warlords, 43, 56, 57, 88
Washington, Booker T., 134

Watts, Richard, 163
Welcome House, 147, 149, 150, 156
Wellesley, 29
West Virginia, 3, 18
wheat, 40
White Russians, 129
White, Edna Edmunds, *see* Edmunds,
    Emma
Whitney, John Hay, 160
Williams, Jack, 57
Wilson, Woodrow, 133
Winds of Heaven, 62, 64; published as
    East Wind: West Wind, 66
Wingless Victory, The, 102
"Wise Mother," 50, 56, 57, 58; *see also*
    Buck, Pearl S., nicknames
Wolcott, Alexander, 75-76
Woman's Home Companion, 88
women's rights, 190
Works, Carie as American of Good, 7
World War I, 38, 130, 131
World War II, 97, 120, 121, 127, 136,
    146, 190, 193

worldwide depression, 92; *see also* Great
    Depression
Wu, Madame, in *Pavilion of Women*,
    141
Wyatt, Jane, 103
Yangtse River, 6, 20, 30, 71
Yaukey family homes, Kobe, 58;
    Shanghai, 60; Fall River,
    Massachusetts, 100
Yaukey, Anne, 86, 87, 88, 100
Yaukey, Grace, visit from Pearl, 86; liv-
    ing in America, 100; knowledge of E.
    Hocking, 172; last visit to Pearl, 182;
    see also Sydenstricker, Grace
Yaukey, Jesse, 51
Yehonala, *see* Empress Dowager Tz'u
    Hsi
Yellowstone Park, 157
Yen, James, 131, 132
Yoder, Lloyd, 148, 150
Yoder, Viola, 148, 150
youth, motivating (footnote on), 136
YWCA Conference at Bryn Mawr, 36